PORTHGAIN & ABEREIDDI

A CENTURY OF INDUSTRY

PETER B. S. DAVIES

MERRIVALE

All rights reserved. No part of this publication may be reproduced, stored in a retrieval system or transmitted in any form or by any means electronic, photocopying, recording or otherwise, without the prior permission of the author.

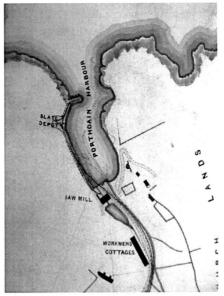

Plan of Porthgain from map of proposed
Barry Island Railway 1850.

Copyright: Peter B. S. Davies 2009

First Published 2004 (ISBN 0 9536982 3 8)
Second (Revised) Edition 2007 (ISBN 0 9536982 5 4)

Third (Revised and Enlarged) Edition 2009
ISBN 978 0 9536982 7 1

Acknowledgements

I wish to express my gratitude to the staffs of the National Library of Wales, National Museums and Galleries of Wales, South Glamorgan Record Office, Pembrokeshire Reference Library and, particularly, Pembrokeshire Record Office, for their help in providing access to the various documents and photographs in their possession. I also wish to thank Thelma Salmon and her late husband Lyndon for permitting me access to surviving company records.

I am grateful to the following organizations and individuals for allowing me to use photographs from their collections: Roy Lewis (9, 12, 14, 18, 23, 40); Mervyn Jones (11, 21, 22, 29, 34); National Museums and Galleries of Wales (13, 18, 26, 30, 31, 32); St. David's & Dewisland Historical Society (16); Pembrokeshire Museums (19, 20, 24); Mary Davies (38).

The people of Porthgain and Abereiddi, many of them friends from my schooldays, have over the years provided much valuable information on the past. To them I express my thanks: I hope they will recognize the names of their fathers and grandfathers and other relatives included among the quarrymen who, after all, are the real heroes of the story of Porthgain and Abereiddi. Others who have provided valuable assistance include Roy Lewis, Chris and Brenda Taylor and George Harries.

Finally to my father and Mr. Crone who first aroused the interest of a young schoolboy in the fascinating story of Porthgain and its industries; but for them this book would never have been written.

The revised and enlarged Third Edition contains information not included in previous editions. For much of this I am indebted to Keith Edwards , who drew my attention to the Stephenson and Alexander archives which are held at the South Glamorgan Record Office. These throw new light on the otherwise little documented last decade of the Nineteenth Century.

Published by Merrivale, St. David's.
Printed by Dimond Press, Pembroke.

Cover: Porthgain village from south c. 1930.

Porthgain & North-west Pembrokeshire

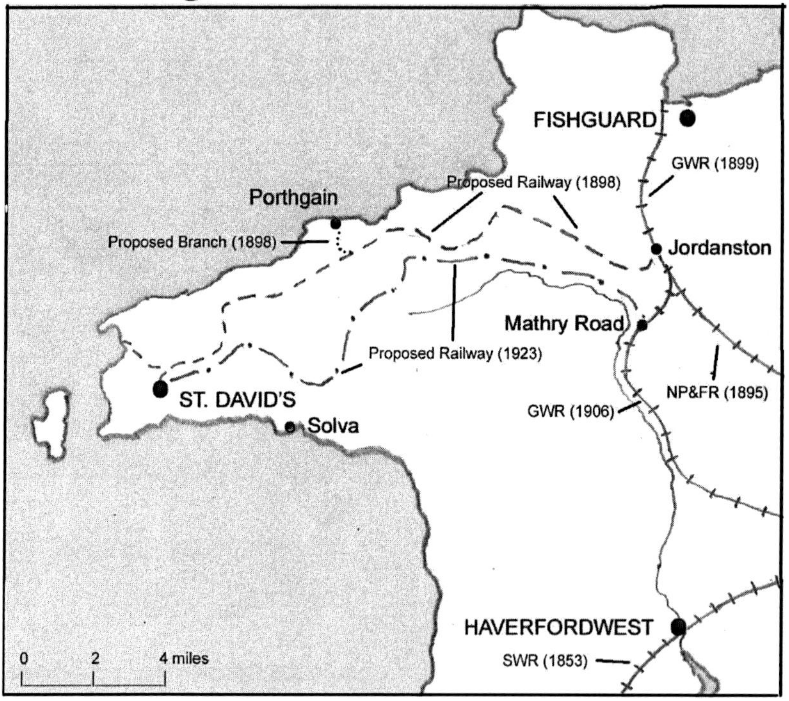

FISHGUARD

GWR (1899)

Proposed Railway (1898)

Porthgain

Proposed Branch (1898)

Jordanston

Mathry Road

Proposed Railway (1923)

ST. DAVID'S

Solva

GWR (1906)

NP&FR (1895)

HAVERFORDWEST

SWR (1853)

0   2   4 miles

1. The Granite Quarries at Penclegyr c. 1960. The roofless buildings at the head of the incline to the lower quarry were the quarry workshops and stores.

Contents

	A Place Where Time Stood Still	7
I	As It Was	13
II	Early Days	15
III	The Age of Slate	20
IV	Slate, Brick and Granite..............	33
V	A Decade of Change	44
VI	The Years of Prosperity	56
VII	The Great War	68
VIII	The Final Phase	71
IX	Aftermath	82
	Porthgain Exports	87
	Bibliography	88

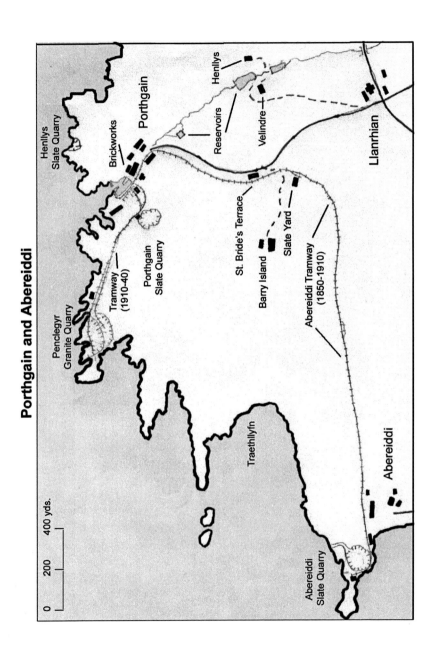

A Place Where Time Stood Still
Porthgain (1930-1950)

Porthgain is a strange place, a place of memories of an age of industry. The harbour, which once brought it prosperity, remains, with the giant red-brick bins clinging to the hill above. The huge, recently re-roofed machinery shed stands in the centre of the village. The slate workshops and the brick kilns have long vanished, as have the stone crushers, the tramways and engine sheds. But the houses of the workmen are still here, and, above all, the people; for most of the cottages are still occupied by the families of the men who once laboured here.

A few of the older inhabitants can still recall Porthgain as it once was. Chimneys belched smoke, the fine grey dust from the crushers shrouded the village. The harbour was full of ships loading chippings, engines strained to haul trucks laden with stone to feed the insatiable appetites of the crushers; but in 1931 it all ended.

My earliest memories are of the late 1930s, when, as a young boy, I lived in the nearby village of Llanrhian where my father was headmaster of the Church School. On summer evenings my father and I would sometimes set out on the mile long walk along the track which ran past Velindre and the quarry reservoirs, and then follow the path down the valley leading to Porthgain. At the entrance to the village we would join the dusty grey road which led from Llanrhian. Beside this was the track bed of the 3 foot gauge railway, which in the last century had brought slate from the quarry at Abereiddi to Porthgain Harbour. From here we would follow the self-contained standard gauge line, on which ran the steam cranes which were used in loading and unloading the ships.

The line ran past the row of cottages known as 'The Street'. At the Company Office we would pause to see if the Manager was in. Usually he was, but if the place was empty we would climb the hill opposite to Sunny Bank where he lived. If not in his office, he was almost certain to be found in his garden – the quarrymen were all great gardeners – or tending his bees. In any case we almost invariably ended up at the office.

A tall, gaunt Irishman, Achilles Stephen Daunt Crone had come to Porthgain in its heyday at the beginning of the century. Since the quarry had closed he had acted as caretaker, looking after and repairing the machinery, waiting and hoping for the day when the quarry would come to life again. In the dank, dark office, cluttered with ledgers and papers, I would listen to them talking of the old days – my father had come to Llanrhian in the 1920s – and of the hopes for the future. I listened, but my thoughts were elsewhere, anticipating the moment when we would set out to accompany the manager on his nightly tour of the works.

2. Porthgain village from south, mid 1950s. 'The Street' is on the left, with the Company Office in front of the last cottage. The Machinery Shed is in the centre with 'The Sloop' and 'Sunnyside' on the eight. The brickworks' chimney has been demolished, but the remains of the Crushing Plant are visible on top of the hill on the left, with the Silt Tip to the right of the harbour.

Usually we strolled along the railway track towards the Harbour, passing between the low, black, slate-built workshops on our left and the towering machinery shed with its attendant brick-drying sheds on the right. Most of the Brickworks had vanished, but the gently curving hundred-foot chimney still dominated the scene.

The cobwebbed, low-roofed Slate Workshops were dark and mysterious, every nook and cranny crammed with strange looking pieces of machinery. Built in the middle of the previous century, of the friable local slate, they dated from the earliest days of slate quarrying at Porthgain; already they were beginning to crumble. By contrast, the Machinery Shed opposite was light and airy; in one corner an ancient lorry rusted away. Strongly built of granite from the nearby quarry, the shed, like the rest of the Brickworks, dated from the end of the nineteenth century.

So we would come to the harbour, deserted but for the odd fishing boat. No longer were the *United Stone Firms*' steamers *Porthgain* or *Liscannor* or in later times *River Humber* to be seen loading granite chippings for Bristol or Bridgwater or any one of a score of destinations around the English coast. No longer did the *Ben Rein* call for cargoes for Haverfordwest or the ketch *Portland* on her routine of stones for Minehead, light to Swansea to load coal for Solva or Porthclais and back to Porthgain. Around the time of the First World War there were at times around a dozen boats waiting for their turn to load. Now the two steam cranes stood forlorn and silent, but still ready for action.

3. Porthgain Harbour c. 1960 with Baxter Quay (centre) and Hadfield Quay (right). The Slate Quarry Tunnel entrance is visible at the base of Bin 1. The earliest of the row Were probably Bins 5-10, with Bin 11 (extreme right) the last. The incline to the upper Level was between Bin 1 and the smaller Bin 1A on the left.

Around the harbour were more 3 foot gauge railway lines on which stood rusting metal trams; once they had been used to carry stone from the bins to the waiting ships. One track led into a tunnel, nearly two hundred yards long, which led to the original Porthgain Slate Quarry, and was used to bring out the slate and the shale which was used for making bricks. In the first years of the century the bricks, dark red and much heavier than normal, were used to build the modern harbour and the enormous storage bins, as well as the engine sheds and workshops for the newly developed quarries whose granite-like stone was, by repute, second only in quality to the granite of Aberdeen.

Sometimes, instead of following the tracks to the harbour, we would cross the leat along which flowed water to a waterwheel which had powered the workshops in the early days. We would climb a steep path, coming out near the top of an incline once used to haul coal to the upper level. Nearby were the crushers, their corrugated iron coverings creaking and groaning in the slightest breeze. A pause to check the machinery, then off we would go again, following the line of another 3 foot gauge railway, a hundred feet above the first. This was better still.

Standing on the sidings were a dozen or more battered wooden wagons, some still loaded with massive blocks of stone, frozen where they had stood that Friday in 1931 when the telegram from headquarters had arrived, telling the men to cease work. The tracks, red with rust, led along the cliffs for about a quarter of a mile; one line slanting down through a shallow cutting to the upper quarry; another, parallel, but on the level, to a group of brick buildings. Here was a stationary steam engine, which had once hauled the loaded wagons up the steep incline from the lower level a hundred feet below. More wagons, some partly filled, stood around the quarries. As elsewhere, it seemed the men had finished work for the week and would return on the Monday morning.

Now it was back along the railway. At the top of the cutting, near the weighbridge, we would follow another track which ran towards a brick building standing on the edge of the slate quarry. Its double wooden doors betrayed its purpose; this was the locomotive shed, the Mecca of our pilgrimage.

The shed was double tracked, but by then held only one locomotive, an 0-4-0 tank called *Newport*. Once there had been others; the first *Porthgain* had arrived in 1909, the second *Singapore* some three years later. They had shared the heavy task of moving stone from the quarries to the crushers – sometimes as much as 400 tons per day. The third of the tank engines *Charger* had worked on the lower railway, moving the crushed stone to the quays where the ships waited. By the late 1920s the original engines were worn out, and *Newport* arrived in 1929 to take over the duty of hauling the much reduced output of the quarries to the crushers.

I was allowed to clamber onto the footplate, and Mr. Crone would show me the controls. I could imagine myself the driver of a real engine; this was much better than any model railway. All too soon it would be time to leave. I always hoped for a chance to travel on the engine, but alas she never moved, though she was kept as immaculately as any main line locomotive.

In 1943 we moved to St. David's; soon, as new interests took over, I had forgotten about Porthgain. About this time Mr. Crone died; there was nobody left to take care of the machinery and buildings, and the place started to decay. The hoped-for Monday never came; the works never reopened, not even during the Second World War, when several new quarries were opened locally to provide stone for the airfields at St. David's and Brawdy, and for the Naval Armament Depot at Trecwn. All that happened was the removal of one of the old slate tips for hardcore.

But Mr. Crone's efforts were not entirely in vain. During the early war years, mines were laid along the piers to enable them to be destroyed in the event of invasion. One day a floating mine came bobbing into the harbour. If it had exploded it could have set off the other mines and blown up half the village.

The inhabitants were evacuated to the Workmen's Institute, a corrugated iron building on the edge of the village. Meanwhile Mr. Crone got up steam in one of the cranes, and attached the hook to the mine which he raised carefully onto the quay. Here, after being made safe by the military, it was inspected by one and all.

It was almost ten years before I again visited Porthgain. By then most of the railway lines and machinery had gone, largely for scrap during the war, though one crane still stood forlornly near the office. The roofs of the buildings were collapsing, and there was an air of dereliction about the village. But *Newport* was still there, mouldering away in what was left of the shed; soon she too would be gone. For the last time I clambered aboard the footplate which held so many memories, then came sadly away.

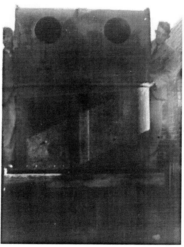

4. *Newport* in roofless loco. shed 1952
Pc Lyn Jones (l), Lloyd Jones (r).

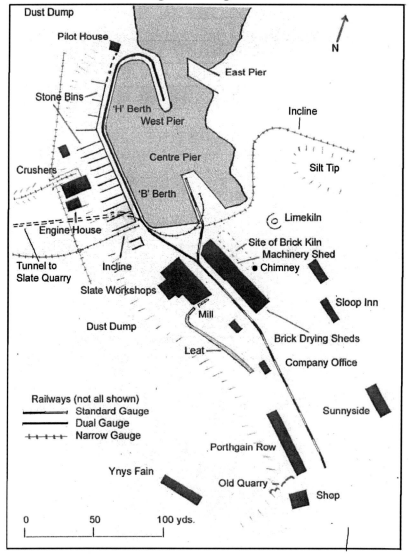

I; As it Was
Porthgain & Abereiddi (1800-1840)

Few visitors came to Porthgain during the early years of the nineteenth century. Most who travelled between Fishguard and St. David's took the high road which passed through Croesgoch. Richard Fenton did visit the church a mile up the valley at Llanrhian, itself a hamlet of manor house, mill and a handful of cottages. None of those who wrote of their journeys passed through Porthgain.

There was no reason why they should come. At that time, long before the first harbour was built, the narrow inlet of Porthgain was a tidal creek, perhaps not unlike the Abercastle of today, with its tidal limit roughly opposite the modern Sloop Inn.

To the east the land formed part of the Henllys Estate, then owned by the Bishop of St. David's. A solitary cottage occupied the site of the inn; nearer the sea was a limekiln. Across the valley the land belonged to Barry Island (Ynys Barri) a large farm, owned by the wealthy Le Hunte family of Artramont, County Wexford, and occupied by William Davies. It was equally desolate, with perhaps a couple of fishermen's cottages at Ynys Fain (Penrallt) and nearby another kiln.

The limekilns, in which Porthgain's earliest industry was carried on, were responsible for what little trade there was. It was in these kilns that limestone was burnt to obtain lime for neutralizing the acid soils of the locality; it was an industry which was already several centuries old. John Williams, who farmed Trearched, was in the late eighteenth century concerned with maintaining a right of way to transport lime and culm along the only road to Porthgain, a track which passed through Henllys land.

One or two fishermen would presumably have kept their small boats at Porthgain. Otherwise there would have been the occasional sloop with its cargo of culm or limestone from the south of the county; craft like the *Royal Oak,* owned by William Davies, and *Ranger*, at one time owned by John Williams. Sometimes, maybe, they would have loaded corn for Bristol, though it was Abercastle which had the only real export trade in agricultural products along the coast between St. David's and Fishguard.

About a mile and a half to the south-west, at the opposite end of the marshy valley separating Barry Island from the rest of the parish, its sands formed from the soft black slate, is the broad beach of Abereiddi. A huddle of cottages, homes to fishermen and workers on the land, and a couple of limekilns, built of the local black slate, stood near its southern end. On the higher ground above the hamlet were a few scattered cottages. Beyond, where a tiny stream cascaded over the cliff was Abereiddi Mill.

To this exposed and hazardous beach (unlike Porthgain there was no shelter to be found here) would have come the odd sloop with its cargo of culm or limestone for Porth Eiddi and the other nearby farms, and for Trevaccoon, the local mansion. That was all, apart from the clandestine cargoes of spirits and tobacco which, from time to time, were landed nearby. The Abereiddi men were, it is said, well known to the Excisemen.

At the opposite end of the parish lay the much larger village of Trefin. Its straggling street stood above the rocky cove of Aberfelin with its mill and the customary limekiln. On the cliffs to the east was a small quarry, owned by the wealthy Harries family of Trevaccoon, known as Trwyn Llwyd. It was reputedly the source of the slate used in 1786 for roofing the church at Llanrhian.

St. David's, the nearest major settlement, lay some five miles to the southwest of Abereiddi; Fishguard and the market town of Haverfordwest were more than twice that distance. For the inhabitants of the parish of Llanrhian the land and the sea provided their only sources of livelihood.

By the mid eighteenth century small scale slate quarrying was being carried on in the locality. A lease dated 1752 refers to the carriage of slates from Aberpwll, a mile west of Abereiddi, to Llanunwas near Solva. In 1811 the geologist, Professor of Chemistry at Cambridge, John Kidd described perhaps the most significant of these early quarries. The *St. David's Slate Quarry* was located in the cliffs at Porth Lleuog, north of Whitesands Bay. The slate was said to be of poor quality, but was being used locally for roofing purposes.

This quarry is marked on a recently republished Ordnance Survey map, based on a survey of 1820, as are several others on the coast near Fishguard. Although the area around Llanrhian is mapped in some detail, no quarries are shown at Abereiddi, Porthgain or Trwyn Llwyd.

Porthgain and Abereiddi remained, as they had been for centuries, two havens of tranquillity, a tranquillity shattered briefly by the French Invasion of 1797 on nearby Pencaer. But, within half a century, the Industrial Revolution was to arrive and change irrevocably these two remote communities.

It was Abereiddi which saw the first awakening of this new age. In 1827 a sloop called the *Jane* of St. David's was registered at Milford. The sole owner was George Propert, slate merchant, of Abereiddi; he was to play a significant part in the coming of industry to the village. No leases or agreements for this period have been discovered, but perhaps quarrying at Trwyn Castell, at least on a small scale, had already begun.

II; Early Days
Abereiddi (1838-1850)

What was to become one of the most remarkable industrial complexes in the whole of Wales began, it is said, in 1838. On 25th October of that year, George Le Hunte granted a 21 year lease to John Jones of Trefin, slater, to quarry for slate and slabs on land forming part of Barry Island; two other local men, William John Ward of Cryglas, St. David's, and Evan Williams of Fishguard, were to act as guarantors of the agreement. However in September 1841 the lease was surrendered.

The Tithe Map for the parish of Llanrhian, dated 1840, shows the quarry at Trwyncastell, though no details are marked. The owner of the quarries is named as George Le Hunte and the occupier is given as James Morgans – the farmer of Barry Island. The area of the quarries was a little over 2¼ acres. A single cottage is shown on the hillside, but there are no other buildings north of the stream. At Porthgain there are no houses on Barry Island land, the only building being the present Sloop Inn on Henllys property. No quarries are shown at Porthgain or Trwyn Llwyd.

The census of 1841 would suggest that any quarrying that was taken place was on a relatively small scale. Lodging with William Watts, farmer, at Abereiddi was seventy years old George Propert a 'Superintendent of Slate Quarry'. William Jones, slater, lived in the village, and there were two others in nearby Porth Eiddi.

In the same year Le Hunte leased the Llanrian Slate Quarries to a group of London businessmen – Benjamin Hill, Robert Norman and John Barclay. It was this company which transformed the original small-scale workings into a thriving concern. They erected various workshops and built a row of seven cottages nearby to house the workmen. They also acquired the lease of the existing Trwyn Llwyd Slate Quarries at Trefin from Samuel Harries of Trevaccoon.

The Abereiddi Slate Quarry occupied land near Trwyn Castell on the northern side of the bay. The entrance to the quarry was along a track some fifty feet above sea level, which led to a platform where the slate workshops and other buildings associated with the quarry were erected.

In the early days, slate was quarried from galleries cut into the cliff face above the platform; the waste being tipped directly into the sea. As quarrying developed, it became necessary to excavate a pit a short distance from the sea to reach the bulk of the slate. Inclines were built connecting to these lower galleries, by means of which the slate and waste were removed. At first the inclines were worked by horses, but by 1848 a steam engine had been introduced for the purpose.

In March of that year the company was apparently in difficulties. The *Pembrokeshire Herald* announced a sale was to take place on 3rd April, under the execution of the Sheriff against the goods of Mr. John Barclay, of all the stock of slates and flags at Abereiddi and Trwyn Llwyd, as well as all the machinery and equipment at the quarries. However these problems seem to have been overcome as, in the following year, the three men were able to re-negotiate the lease.

To Evan Evans, aged 34, a native of Llandwrog, Caernarvonshire, the future in 1851 must have seemed full of promise. A few years previously he had come to Abereiddi to work in the newly opened slate quarries; he had prospered and was already a slate quarryman employing eight others. Home was one of the row of seven single-storey, two-roomed cottages which the company had built for its workmen at the northern end of the bay. Here he lived with his Irish wife Catherine, their two young daughters and two quarrymen lodgers.

In the cottages lived a total of sixteen quarrymen; fathers and sons and others who lodged with them. Men, mostly in their twenties and early thirties, almost all had been born in North Wales. One of the oldest was 51 years old William Jones, the youngest his 12 years old son Thomas, a slater. William, exceptionally, had been born in Portsmouth, though his wife was Caernarvonshire born as was Thomas; an older son William Thomas (junior) had been born in Llanwerin in Montgomery, and there were three other children.

In the old settlement at the southern end of the bay and in nearby Cyffredin and Porth Eiddi lived others who worked in the quarries. But they were mostly local; men like St. David's born John Evans aged 67, and 23 years old John Thomas who had been born in Llanrhian parish. At the farm in Abereiddi, owned and occupied by William Watts, lodged two senior officials of the quarry – Griffith Jones from South Wales, the agent, and his clerk John Keith, a native of Aberdeen. In Trefin lived another twenty or so slaters and quarrymen who presumably worked at Trwyn Llwyd; most came from North Wales.

The railway had not yet reached Pembrokeshire, and the slate could only be exported long distances by sea. But there was no harbour at Abereiddi. In those days coastal vessels were run ashore at high tide, loaded with slate, then floated off on the next high tide. Only small sloops carrying perhaps 30 tons could use the beach, and then only during summer months when the weather was calm. It was a hazardous business as the owners of *Weasel* of London found to their cost. On 23rd August, 1838, she was wrecked by a gale at Abereiddi, though fortunately her crew were saved.

Records of shipping are sparse. However the *Carmarthen Journal* of 10th October, 1838, records the departure of the *Mary Anne* from 'Aberithe' for

London. The cargo book of the Abercastle sloop *Hope* refers to two cargoes of 23 tons of slate being carried from Abereiddi to Pater (Pembroke Dock) the freightage being 2s.0d. per ton. In 1847 she carried a cargo of slates to Ayr, freightage being 12s.6d. per ton.

To build a harbour at Abereiddi was not practicable. However, less than two miles away was the relatively sheltered haven of Porthgain. It could easily be developed. Between Abereiddi and Porthgain ran a valley which would provide a suitable route for the construction of a tramway for transporting the slate to the harbour. By 1851 schemes for both harbour and railway were in progress.

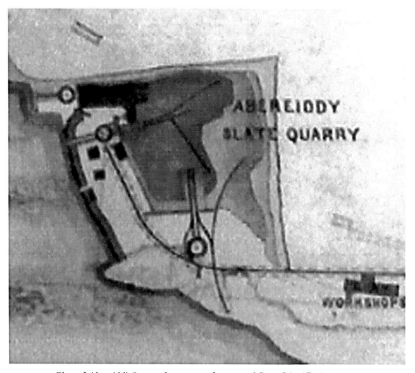

Plan of Abereiddi Quarry from map of proposed *Barry Island Railway* 1850.

The original plans for the *Barry Island Railway* – a 3 foot gauge line between Abereiddi and Porthgain – have recently come to light. They show the Slate Quarry at Abereiddi in some detail. Considerable development had already taken place, with the working galleries extending well below the level of the intended railway. The system of inclines and tramways connecting the various levels, together with the winding engines, is clearly shown. The positions of workshops and other quarry buildings are also indicated.

The extent of the quarry shows that a great deal of extraction had taken place by 1850. The vast bulk of the slate must have been shipped out from the beach; obviously Abereiddi had been busy exporting slates during the 1840s and probably for some time before that. Certainly the references to slates being shipped to London before the lease of October 1838 came into effect would suggest a significant quarry already existed.

The row of cottages at Abereiddi is not marked, though at Porthgain 'The Street' is labelled as Workmen's Cottages. At the latter place a pier, slate depot and sawmill with mill pond are depicted, though there is no indication of any quarrying having taken place nearby. At this stage Slate Yard is only a passing loop on the line and the nearby Scotch Houses are not shown.

5. The Magazine at Abereiddi Quarry dates from the early days of slate quarrying.

The railway began at the Engine House. For a short distance it ran south beside a row of small sheds where the slate was dressed. It then curved eastwards, past more workshops and the circular Powder House, and above the row of workmen's cottages. Here, at a double-tracked Slate Depot, the finished slates were stored before despatch by rail. For almost a mile the line (with one passing loop) continued in this direction, more or less on the level, along a platform cut into the hillside. It then turned north along the valley bottom, crossing the lane leading from Llanrhian to Barry Island at a place which became known as Slate Yard. From here it ran downhill along the valley bottom to the western side of the harbour at Porthgain.

The rail contractor in charge of the construction was Robert Irving, a 22 years old Scotsman. Working under him were half a dozen rail labourers; the latter all lived in or around Abereiddi, but Irving lived on the western side of Porthgain, in one of a handful of cottages (presumably 'The Street') scarcely deserving the title of hamlet.

By 1848, Messrs. Hill, Norman and Barclay, trading as the *Barry Island Slate & Slab Company*, had devised a plan to build a proper harbour at Porthgain. In 1851 they obtained from the *Commissioners of Her Majesty's Woods, Forests, Land, Revenues, Works & Buildings* the conveyance of land between the High and Low Water Marks at Porthgain.

By the time of the census, work had commenced on improving the harbour. This involved the construction of two short, stone piers at the harbour entrance, providing shelter for the shipping within. Inside the western pier was a simple wharf with a crane for loading slate onto the ships; nearby, at the end of the tramway, was a Slate Depot for storing slate awaiting shipment. Near the high water mark the plan shows a workshop for cutting and planing the slate. The slate would hardly have been carried from Abereiddi for finishing, suggesting that quarrying at Porthgain might already have started.

Half a mile up the valley towards Llanrhian stood the imposing residence of Velindre, home to yet another Scotsman – John Hyslop, mineral agent, who was in charge locally for the London-based owners. They had plans for further expansion, and they were based on Porthgain.

The new harbour at Porthgain and the tramway would undoubtedly help the company in its competition with the quarries of North Wales. However, the black Abereiddi slate was not of the best quality; it tended to be porous and was not long lasting. But at Porthgain itself, within a hundred yards of the harbour, lay slate reputed to be of superior quality. It was on the development of this that the future of the company depended.

III; The Age of Slate
Abereiddi & Porthgain (1850-1890)

Throughout most of the 1850s developments continued apace; but now they were centred on Porthgain as well as Abereiddi. For half a century, at least intermittently, horse-drawn trams laden with black slate would continue to trundle along the two miles of track from Abereiddi quarry, past the storage area at Slate Yard, to the harbour at Porthgain. No steam locomotive ever ran along this line – production did not merit it.

Meanwhile, a new quarry was opened about 150 yards west of the harbour. The quarry was in the form of a roughly circular pit which was eventually about 100 yards in diameter. From here the slate was transported to workshops near the quay where it was trimmed to size. The new quarry had the advantage of being near the harbour and the slate was supposedly of better quality than that obtained from Abereiddi.

At first extraction was relatively easy, but as the pit grew deeper an incline was constructed on the northern side of the quarry to give access to the working levels. The wagons, laden with slate, were hauled up this incline (originally by means of a horse-drawn whim) before being moved to the top of a second incline, then lowered by another horse whim to the workshops on the quay. It was costly in terms of time and labour, especially as for every 8 tons raised from the quarry floor only 1 ton of usable slate was obtained. The remainder was taken by rail to waste tips on the cliff top north of the quarry.

On the plateau, 100 feet above the quay, the *Barry Island Slate and Slab Company,* who then owned the quarry, erected various buildings associated with the quarry; workshops and stores and stables for the horses. In the valley were more workshops for trimming the slate, their machinery powered by a waterwheel served by a leat from the stream which flowed down the valley.

The new operations were on a far greater scale than those originally carried out at Abereiddi alone. Slate quarrying was a highly labour-intensive industry, requiring many skilled workmen, most of whom had to be brought in from other areas. To house them the company built two rows of cottages at Porthgain; Porthgain Row, locally known as 'The Street', of five cottages in the valley, and another row of seven, Pentop Terrace, on the hill overlooking the harbour; both were essentially similar to the row at Abereiddi. There were also a few rather larger houses for the more senior employees; all these, as well as the quarry buildings themselves, were on Barry Island land. In addition there were five houses, built back-to-back, officially called St. Bride's Terrace, but known locally as 'Scotch Houses' on the Llanrhian road at Slate Yard.

In spite of the considerable expenditure, the method of working was old fashioned and inefficient. Apart from one steam engine employed at the Abereiddi quarry, all the winding, hauling and pumping – much of it unnecessary – was carried out literally by horse-power.

The local slate could never hope to compete with that of North Wales in terms of quality – Abereiddi slate had a life expectancy of about forty years, perhaps a quarter of that of the best Caernarvonshire slate. However, with the Porthgain quarry within a stone's throw of the harbour, while many of the Caernarvonshire quarries were several miles from the sea, it should have had the edge in terms of cost. Much of that advantage was thrown away by the method of production. Every ton of slate, and many more tons of waste, was laboriously raised from the working levels to the quarry rim, before the slate was lowered again to the quay. As the pit grew deeper, so the costs of production increased. Over the next quarter of a century tens of thousands of tons of slate and waste were handled in this manner. As Herbert Birch (the man who eventually took charge of the concern) pointed out, most of this could have been avoided if the quarry had been opened into the hill from the valley at Porthgain itself.

6. Flangeless wheels found during excavations at Porthgain c. 2000 suggest that early tramways were Plateways rather than Railways.

Records of quarrying for the nineteenth century are rare; but a letter book of the *Barry Island Slate Company*, covering the period from January 1857 to March 1859, has survived. It appears that previously Abereiddi had been worked under licence by the Irvings, but (to the relief of the owners) they had recently withdrawn from the quarry.

In 1857 all three quarries were in operation, Abereiddi being much the most successful. During August it produced slates valued at £160 at a cost of £60; the corresponding figures for Porthgain were £48 and £20, and for Trwynllwyd £21 and £11. The results from Porthgain were particularly disappointing due, it was said, to the fall in sales of slate slabs.

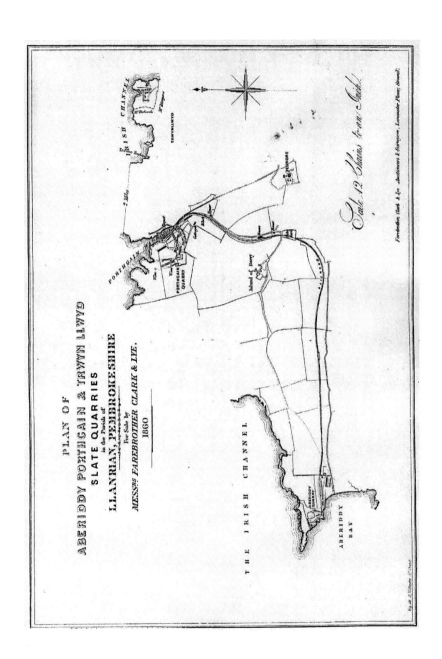

There were comments on the cost of labour at Porthgain, where H. John received the highest wage of 2s.6d. per day while three others (James Lewis, W. Harries and E. Jones) were paid at least 2s.0d.. At the much more productive Abereiddi James Price was, at 2s.4d., the highest paid, only one other man, H. Williams, being paid as much as 2s.0d..

In charge at 'Trwyn' was Price Roberts; at Porthgain William Pritchard; while at Abereiddi Evan Evans was superintendent quarryman. Pritchard was considered largely to blame for complaints by including poor quality old stock from Porthgain among cargoes of slate for export. At Abereiddi a project for sinking a shaft, presumably to allow access to a new working gallery, was to proceed.

A survey carried out by Evan Evans at Abereiddi suggests that the quarry then measured about 400ft. by 220ft. and was about 100ft. deep. According to John Barclay it was estimated that profits of about £70,000 would be made over a period of about six years by working the reserves.

During 1857 some thirty shipments of slates or slate slabs are recorded as being exported from Porthgain. Most were local; ten to Milford, six to Pembroke Dock. In South Wales one or more shipments were sent to Swansea, Newport, Cardiff and Neath. The most valuable cargo was worth £140 carried in *Brothers* of Cardigan to Portsmouth; the total value of the cargoes being in excess of £1,420. Tonnages are seldom mentioned, though *Connivum* of Dinas carried 42 tons of 'seconds' valued at £40 to Dundee. Elsewhere in Scotland there were two shipments to Nairn and one to Fraserburgh. There was a single cargo of slates to Wexford in Ireland.

Altogether seventeen ships are recorded as carrying slate from Porthgain. Almost all were locally owned sloops; *Britannia* of Solva, *Queen of Trumps* of Fishguard, *True Bess* of St. David's, could carry thirty or forty tons; *Margaret* of Abercastle about twenty.

Most shipments were made during the early part of the year, by autumn demand for slates had diminished significantly. The reason for loss of customers in South Wales was apparently the poor quality of some of the slates and the numbers which were broken. In the north of England and Scotland, the main problem was the cost of transport compared with that from North Wales. Freightage to Liverpool was quoted as 10s.6d. per ton. Sales to Bristol and Gloucester were lost because the quarries were unable to supply enough slates of large size.

In April 1858 the quarrymen ceased work as they had not been paid. The company secretary blamed the delay in payment on the illness of one of the proprietors. Work was resumed, largely by contract, but by July the men were again threatening to strike.

For the nine months to June 1858 sales amounted to some £460, but unsold stocks were accumulating and there was an urgent need for disposing of the surplus. Some success was achieved by selling slates for cash; in the four weeks to 23rd September over £400 was raised in this way and two weeks' wages were paid to the men. During the year some twenty shipments of slate were made, including one to Nairn and two to Liverpool. Newport (Gwent) received five cargoes, Cardiff two and Swansea one – the remainder were to a variety of destinations in South Pembrokeshire.

On 1st September it was decided to close Porthgain immediately, but retaining contracts at Abereiddi as far as possible. By November the pumping engines were in need of repair if the working levels at Porthgain and Abereiddi were not to be flooded. By early 1859 the Abereiddi contracts had been cancelled and there was grave danger of inundation as the sea wall had not been properly repaired.

Within months the company was declared bankrupt and, in October 1860, it was put up for sale though it was not immediately sold. The sale particulars refer to the steam engine at Abereiddi, a horse whim at Trwyn Llwyd and three horse whims and a horse pump at Porthgain. Not described are two engines mentioned in the Letter Book of 1857-59; "They have been at work since the beginning of 1853 – they are very economical in the use of fuel." The accompanying plan shows the railway linking Abereiddi to Porthgain, as well as the quarries and their associated inclines. Also shown is a tunnel apparently linking the quarry at Porthgain with a point on the coast known as Aber Tunnell.

By 1861 almost all the North Wales quarrymen had left and only a dozen slate workers remained in the parish. Some of the quarrymen's cottages were empty, others were occupied by the wives and families of men who had left to seek work elsewhere. Evan Evans still lived in Abereiddi and is described in the census as 'slate agent'. There were only three slaters living in Abereiddi and two in Porthgain. At the latter William Pritchard, a native of Beddgelert, was agent for the slate works while Northumberland born James Jack was manager. The company mansion at Velindre was vacant.

The 47 years old manager had lived in Pembrokeshire for many years though not always in Porthgain. His older children had been born in Haverfordwest, the others in St. Dogwells, the parish containing the Sealyham Slate Quarry. The Scottish millwright Alexander Hardie's five years old youngest son had been born in Haverfordwest. The slaters from North Wales had gone, those who remained were mostly local men like Llanrhian born William Richards and Henry Rees, both of Abereiddi, and William Waters, a native of St. David's, who lived in Porthgain. The wives who had stayed while their husbands went away to seek employment were, like Martha Rees and Eleanor Rees of Abereiddi, local girls.

For those employed in the quarries the work was hard and the hours long; and it was dangerous work. In July 1862 William Tew was killed at the Porthgain Slate Works by a stone which fell on his head; he left a widow and three children.

Prospects were nevertheless about to improve. Within months the quarries were purchased by Messrs. Hewett and Grierson. They had plans for improving the harbour by constructing a new pier; they had plans for providing more power by erecting a windmill and building a mill dam to create a new reservoir.

7. Velindre, the home of the Company Manager at Llanrhian.

At that time the operation was known as the *Porthgain Slate and Slab Quarries and Steam Mills*. A letter written in June 1864 on behalf of the owners Hewett & Co. to Henry Williams, master and owner of the sloop *Hope* of Abercastle, complained of lack of cooperation with regard to carriage of cargoes of slate. It also demanded payment for obstruction of the harbour.

The letter confirms that the pier had been built and the harbour otherwise improved. Little else came of the proposals, though a dam was built near Velindre; eventually three reservoirs were provided – two by damming the stream near Velindre, the third being a smaller mill pond just above the village.

Most of the exports would probably have been carried in local ships. The *Crew Lists and Log Books* for the Ports of Milford and Cardigan (though incomplete) give some idea of the activity of the quarries during the latter part of the nineteenth century. In 1863 only half a dozen shipments are recorded to destinations including Carmarthen, Gloucester and Dundalk; in 1864 there was only a single cargo for Bristol.

During 1864 the quarries were taken over by the *St. Bride's United Slate and Slab Co. Ltd.*. The chief promoter of the new company was John Davies of Narberth, a major shareholder in a number of quarries in the county. At last there was money available to modernize the operation of the quarries. But first there was much rubble to be removed from the working faces and the derelict tramway from Abereiddi to Porthgain to be reopened.

Over the next few years much development was carried out at the three quarries. As was reported in the *Mining Journal* of 22nd February, 1868, the Abereiddi quarry consisted of four galleries, all in good working order and yielding slates of excellent quality at low cost. In the previous month 72,000 slates had been produced and there were ample reserves to last for many years. Trwyn Llwyd was producing slabs of very high quality; output had been small, but could be greatly increased. At Porthgain, which produced both slates and slabs, more expenditure was required to bring the quarry back into full production. The bottom of the quarry needed to be cleared of rubbish and the second gallery extended to allow extraction of slabs from the gallery below. In addition another forty yards of tunnel was needed to allow the removal of rubbish from the third gallery; presumably this is the tunnel marked on the Sale Plan of 1860. When this had been completed – at an estimated cost of £300 – the quarry should be able to produce 50 tons of high quality slab per day at a large profit.

The tunnel was not completed, and the wasteful process of hauling the rubbish from the bottom of the quarry, only for it to be tipped on the clifftop, continued. For the first time steam power was employed at Porthgain, stationary engines being used to work the double-acting inclines by which the slates were raised from the quarry and lowered to the quay. Elsewhere horses continued to be used to pull the trams.

By 1868 trade had improved with shipments of slates to Liverpool (4), Runcorn (3), Gloucester (4) and Bristol (1). More local were single cargoes to Llanelli, Aberystwyth and Milford. In 1869 there were five shipments including one of 'slab stones' to London. The years 1870 and 1871 saw single cargoes to Waterford and 1872 shipments to Pembroke Dock and Milford.

Success proved short lived. Soon the quarry owners were once again in financial difficulties and in 1871 there were barely a dozen quarrymen living in the parish. Manager of the quarries was now Thomas Williams who lived at Norman Terrace (presumably St. Bride's Terrace); the quarry agent William Pritchard of Cwmwdig Water. Both were natives of Caernarvonshire. At Abereiddi lived two quarrymen; in Porthgain itself were six quarrymen; all, like 43 years old James James of Porthgain, were Pembrokeshire born. In Trefin lived seven slaters and quarrymen; most like 44 years old Price Roberts, were originally from North Wales.

Velindre was empty, as was Norman Villa. Only three cottages at Pentop were inhabited, two of them by quarrymen's wives; in Trefin was one house occupied by a slater's wife. Both Henry Rees and Thomas Rees, who lived at Abereiddi, were described as 'quarryman out of employ'. Most of the cottages in the village housed families whose menfolk were not employed in the quarries. Fortunes were once more at a low ebb.

Around 1870 it was proposed to build a railway from Heathfield (where it would link with an intended line from Haverfordwest to Fishguard) to St. David's. Originally a fairly direct route was surveyed. John Davies and his fellow directors suggested the route should be altered to bring the route as near the St. Bride's Quarries as possible, while the coal owners of Roch and Nolton favoured a southern diversion to bring the line nearer to their mines. In the event none of these lines was built.

8. Traethllyfn, in 1876 this was proposed as the site for another slate quarry.

For some time the quarries lay dormant. However in May 1875 it was announced in the local press that the company was reopening all three quarries. By 1876 Thomas Evans, Engineer, of St. David's, writing in the *Mining Journal* could refer to "an excellent quarry near St. David's – the St. Bride's Slate and Slab Quarry – which was started a few months ago."

The company which now owned the quarries was the *St. Bride's Welsh Slate and Slab Company*, again with John Davies as a major shareholder and director. There were plans for further expansion, including the opening of yet another slate quarry at Traethllyfn, on the coast between Abereiddi and Porthgain. This was to be linked by rail, surprisingly to Abereiddi and not to Porthgain. Like so many of the other schemes put forward, nothing came of this particular plan.

In other respects the optimistic forecasts proved, at least for a time, to be justified. On 26th May, 1877, the *Dewsland and Kemes Guardian* was able to announce;

"The St. Bride's Slate Quarries in this neighbourhood (Llanrhian) continue to progress very satisfactorily. Between the 3 quarries, Abereithy, Porthgain and Trwynllwyd, over 300 hands are kept busy and the little hamlet of Porthgain already assumes a busy air for this neighbourhood."

Whit Monday had been declared a general holiday at the quarries. Celebrations were the order of the day. The claim of the number employed is almost certainly an exaggeration (though Herbert Birch later claimed that several hundred men had at one time been employed in the quarries) but perhaps never before had the future seemed brighter. Festivities were however marred by a drunken brawl at Croesgoch, in which Richard Lloyd sustained serious head injuries after being struck by a missile thrown by one of the crowd.

On the afternoon of Wednesday, 13th June, a ceremony took place at Porthgain, attended by a large number of workmen and their families. It recognised the 'amiable relations' which existed between management and workers, the latter presenting a testimonial to the manager, John Davies; "the gentleman who has been chiefly instrumental in re-establishing the work at the Quarries."

No company records survive from this period. However the *Crew Lists and Log Books* give some idea of the trade. In 1877 the destinations included Liverpool (4 shipments), Penarth (2) and Gloucester (1); there were no recorded shipments to local destinations. In 1878 there were three cargoes for London and one each for Shoreham, Runcorn and Liverpool. During the next two years, the 67 ton *Milo* carried five loads of slate to London and one to Newhaven; no other shipments are recorded.

The 'amiable relations' were not to last. Within a short time the company was in serious financial difficulties. In January 1879, according to the *Dewsland and Kemes Guardian*, the workmen were complaining that they had received no pay for three months. With no money coming in, the quarrymen could not afford to pay for food and other necessaries; soon the shopkeepers were forced to withdraw credit from the workers. The quarry-men took the only course open to them and withdrew their labour. It was a difficult decision for the men to make; they had never been active in the Trade Union movement, though some would have remembered the troubles of two decades earlier.

For the workmen and their families it was a time of great deprivation; some decided to leave the area to seek work elsewhere, while others clung on in the hope of the situation improving. The company was equally concerned, and the chairman promised he would personally see that the men were fully paid if they agreed to return to work. Some of the men did return and some of the arrears in wages were paid.

On 8th February John Fraser (the quarry manager) writing in the *Dewsland and Kemes Guardian*, insisted that with three exceptions the men had returned to work. A week later he wrote that only bad weather prevented the shipment of 400 tons of slate. On 1st March he stated that in the previous few days fully laden vessels had sailed for London and Shoreham, and that other vessels were expected when the weather improved. The letter continued;

"In addition to the slate and slab works it is expected we shall shortly see the commencement of granite quarrying in this place. A few gentlemen from London were down last week making an inspection of rocks, the result of which examination is not yet known. It is hoped for the welfare of the neighbourhood that the decision will be favourable."

Whether this refers to Penclegyr is not clear. During the construction of the piers it seems that granite had been obtained from a small quarry where the road from Llanrhian enters the village and this may have been the site under examination.

Another report in the same paper by the local correspondent on 22nd March stated that on the previous Wednesday the quarry tools had been collected and the men dismissed. A letter, signed by over thirty of the men, which was forwarded to company headquarters asked for an explanation for their dismissal and requested payment of the arrears in wages. In April one month's wages were paid and there was promise of further instalments. But work did not resume and before the year was out the *St. Bride's Welsh Slate and Slab Company*, like several of its predecessors, became bankrupt.

In 1880 the quarries were described as being idle. However in March it was reported that the quarries were ready to resume work; the men had been fully paid and the liquidators of the old company had agreed terms. In October the company was advertising that stocks of slates were to be sold off cheaply.

The census of 1881 shows that the quarries were again operating, although on a relatively small scale. At Abereiddi, Lewis Davies was manager of the slate quarries, while Thomas Thomas, aged 44, was described as an engineer. The row of cottages was referred to as 'Little Brighton'; two were occupied by Philip Cronin and Thomas Butler, both Irishmen, who worked in the quarries. Surprisingly the latter had two Irish-born slatemakers as lodgers; his wife Anastasia and their three children, the youngest aged 7, had all been born in Ireland. Three of the other cottages were also occupied by workers at the quarries, and there were two other slaters living elsewhere in the village; all but one were local men.

In Porthgain, four of the cottages in Porthgain Row were occupied by slate quarrymen – all Pembrokeshire born; the fifth housed David Harries, general labourer, who had two quarry employees as lodgers. In Number 6, the one house in the row, lived Samuel Hughes, a native of Bethesda, with his wife, daughter and step-daughter.

By contrast, five of the seven cottages at Pentop were empty; of the others one was occupied by a slate maker. There was only one labourer in the slate quarries at St. Bride's Terrace, though Porthgain born Margaret Williams, engineer's wife, lived in one of the houses. John James, slate quarry foreman, lived in nearby Kenfield House. At Velindre the occupier was away from home. In Trefin, Price Roberts, 54, was now stone quarry manager. In and around the village lived four others who worked in the slate quarries.

The Stephenson & Alexander Papers include a number of reports made in 1880-81 to a concern calling itself the *Pembroke Granite Company* which mention both granite deposits. The suitability of the stone for making setts, kerbs, etc., is extolled, as is the convenient position of the harbour for shipping the product. However nothing seems to have come of this particular scheme.

9. The only known photograph of Porthgain in the Slate Era c. 1880 before the construction of the Brickworks or the modern Harbour. The Winding Engine House is at the top of the Incline, with Workshops (left) and Pentop Terrace (right). In the valley are Porthgain Row with Slate Workshops (centre) and the Slate Depot on the Quay. The Sloop Inn is on the right.

In 1883 the quarries were taken over by the *United Welsh Slate Company*, yet another company in which John Davies was involved. The new company inherited all the property and plant, including two steam engines at Porthgain and one each at Abereiddi and Trwyn Llwyd. The engine at Abereiddi and one of those at Porthgain were fitted with lifting gear, presumably for raising slate and waste from the bottom of the quarries which had become too deep to be worked by the original inclines.

The people of the parish of Llanrhian must have been dubious of yet another prophecy of a brighter future for the quarries from the lips of John Davies. Their fears would have been well justified. According to Herbert Birch, Abereiddi was to remain closed until 1893; accounting for the tramway being marked 'disused' on the 1887 Ordnance Survey map. The evidence of the shipping records suggests that for much the 1880s there was little, if any, activity at Porthgain.

But at last there were good times around the corner, and it was the *United Welsh Slate Company* which was to provide them. But before that happened new leadership was needed, with men of vision who could see that Porthgain had more to offer than just slate.

These new operations were soon to sweep away all the buildings and tramways around the slate quarry at Porthgain. By a fortunate chance it was in 1887 that the 25 inches to 1 mile Ordnance Survey (1st Edition) map of Porthgain and Abereiddi was drawn, showing them at what was virtually the end of the slate age. It was in 1889 that Herbert Birch, the man who was to change the whole outlook of the company, became involved with Porthgain.

Abereiddi c. 1887

31

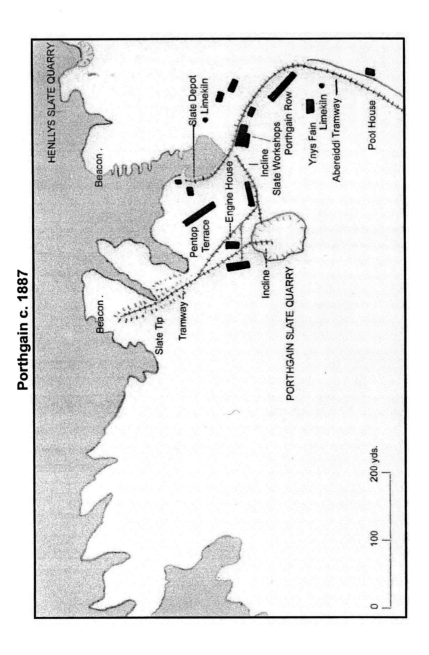

IV; Slate, Brick and Granite
Porthgain & Abereiddi (1889-1900)

"The Pen Top Quarry, although situated only about 160 yards from Porthgain Harbour, had been sunk into the heart of the higher land and not opened from the side of the hill. The situation of the quarry necessitated the hauling up of the refuse 140 feet to the top, and tipping it over the cliff, and also the hauling of the undressed slabs over the top and lowering them in trams to the mills on the wharf. This was one of the most roundabout and laborious plans that could be devised. There was also the immense waste of power in pumping the water from the quarry by means of machinery driven by water-power in the valley."

This was the damning report of the new proprietors of the *United Welsh Slate Company* on the efforts of their predecessors. The account in the *Haverfordwest & Milford Haven Telegraph* of 28th May, 1890, continues:

"One of the first things done by the new company was to drive a tunnel 160 yards long through the hill, thus connecting the quarry with the mills and wharf, and saving endless labour and valuable motive power. The slabs from the quarry and the refuse are now brought by gravitation through the tunnel, which also serves to carry off any water."

A prospectus issued by the company about this time described the Porthgain Quarry as measuring 294ft. by 160ft. and being 130ft. deep. It comprised five galleries and was capable of producing 6,000 tons per annum of high quality slab. In addition, a recently discovered vein of blue roofing slate was also being worked, as well as a 17yd. wide vein of green slate.

Abereiddi Quarry measured about 450ft. by 300ft. and was about 150ft. deep. It consisted of five well-constructed galleries and was capable of producing upwards of 80,000 first quality slates per month. Both quarries were well equipped with plant and machinery, slate sheds and tramways.

The Trwyn Llwyd Quarry was acquired by J. B. Harries who operated it independently for several years producing slate slabs. It had never been directly linked to the rest of the property; although small craft could be loaded directly at the quarry, most of the products were taken by road to the harbour at Porthgain, a cumbersome and costly process. However the company had purchased the Henllys Estate; this included the Henllys Quarry – a cliff quarry about a hundred yards east of Porthgain, It was intended to use this for the production of roofing slates.

Although the problem of transporting the slate and waste material from the Porthgain Quarry was solved by the construction of the tunnel, there still remained the question of what could be done with the waste. Herbert Birch and his colleagues had the answer to this; they would use it to manufacture bricks.

According to a prospectus issued by the company, the Porthgain Brickworks was the only one in Britain which used slate waste for producing bricks. It described the process employed in the works:

"The Slate and Slab debris or waste is conveyed by trams direct from the Quarries and Mills to the crushing pans, where it passes under heavy rollers and through sieves, until finely pulverised, after which it is moistened and thoroughly kneaded in a Mixer, from which it passes to the presses and comes out a finished brick. The machines now erected turn out 50,000 per week, but the capacity of the main plant is upwards of 80,000 per week. From the machine house the bricks pass direct to a large Hoffman Kiln, which has capacity for 200,000 bricks, and can turn out 50,000 per week. This Kiln by greatly economising heat, and burning slowly, ensures the bricks more even colour and greater hardness."

10. Porthgaim Slate Quarry from east.

The enormous machine house, two storeys high and constructed of local granite, was erected on waste ground directly opposite the slate mills at the head of the harbour; at its eastern end was a low range of drying sheds. The Hoffman Kiln, divided into four sections in which the bricks were in turn loaded, fired, cooled and removed, was built immediately north of the machine shed. Towering above all was the hundred foot high chimney of the kiln.

The *Haverfordwest and Milford Haven Telegraph* of 8th March, 1890, announced that the tunnel from the Pen Top Quarry had been completed, and that production of slate slabs would begin the following week. The brick machine house had been fitted out, and it was hoped to commence making bricks in the near future. By May the brick making plant was said to be in full operation – at that stage the bricks were being burnt in open kilns pending the completion of the Hoffman kiln.

About a quarter of a mile west of the harbour, in the cliffs at Penclegyr, was stone said to be second in hardness only to the granite of Aberdeen. This was referred to by the company as 'Syenite Granite' though strictly it was andesite. For the first time it was to be exploited commercially; in July 1889 the company was advertising in the local press for young boys to become apprentices for the making of granite setts.

At first the main products of the quarry were building stone and granite setts for paving streets, for which its hard wearing properties made it ideal. Initially the sett makers' chips and defective stone were tipped over the cliff, while the blocks and setts were taken in horse-drawn trams to the top of the incline leading to the quay. However, within a short time a crusher was installed to deal with the waste which was broken into chippings suitable for roadmaking. After crushing to the required size, these were stored in the yard alongside the harbour while awaiting shipment. According to Mr. Crone, then quarry manager, in a letter to Company Headquarters dated 13th August, 1925, the original crusher had been sited in old buildings near the Institute. He recalled that around 1900 a tramway had run from the site of the later locomotive shed past Penrallt to a point above the crusher.

With the construction of the tunnel to the slate quarry, the tramways and many of the associated buildings on the upper level became redundant. The tramways were dismantled and replaced by a line from the granite quarry at Penclegyr, running past the sites of the later weighbridge and loco shed, to the top of the incline to the harbour. At the beginning of the twentieth century, when the storage bins were built along the quay, new crushers were installed above them. The branch to the original crusher was replaced by others leading to the new crushers. As on the previous system the wagons were horse-drawn.

The powerful traction engine, previously used as a winding engine at Pentop, was moved to the valley where it was used to power the original stone crusher. The fixed engine from Abereiddi had been installed in the brickmaking plant. A new boiler was intended for use for sawing and planing in the slab mill which could be worked by steam or water power. There were in all six steam engines and boilers available as well as the water wheel. There was however need for a powerful steam crane for loading at the harbour.

One of the problems at Porthgain was a powerful tidal surge which, under certain conditions, swept into the harbour. A possible solution, suggested by George Owen Williams of Cross House, St. David's, was that a series of parallel timbers (arranged like a Venetian blind) should be attached to a buoy moored outside the harbour in order to break up the waves. In April 1890, Mr. Williams carried out an underwater survey of the approaches to the harbour. In connection with this he advised against the practice of tipping slate waste over the cliff, as this would cause further silting of the harbour.

In March 1890 the company purchased Trinity Quay, Solva, for £505. It was intended to use the site for transferring cargo to larger vessels. There were elaborate schemes for setting up a shipping line linking Porthgain and other West Wales harbours with Bristol, Liverpool and even London. Vessels coming to Porthgain to load cargo were to import coal for resale via a depot to be set up at Neyland.

The company did in fact acquire three steamers; *Maggie Ann*, *Edith* and *Marion*, as well as a steam tug *Ernest*. The latter was to be used to assist vessels berthing at Porthgain, a harbour which was notoriously difficult to enter for sailing vessels. *Maggie Ann* (it was intended to rename her *Llanrian*) foundered off Abereiddi on 18th December, 1890, when laden with road stone for Southampton. Described by the company as 'almost new' and capable of carrying 160 tons of cargo, she had originally been built in 1868, though later rebuilt and lengthened.

The 1891 census lists some forty men living in Porthgain and Abereiddi as quarrymen or brickworkers of various descriptions, apart from other tradesmen who were presumably employed there. In its prospectus the company had claimed to own fifty-eight substantially built houses and cottages. At Porthgain there were six men associated with slate quarrying, ten with stone quarrying and nine with the brickworks. In and around Abereiddi lived ten stone-quarry workers and one brickmaker, but nobody directly linked with slate quarrying. At this time Abereiddi Quarry remained closed. The local workmen would have had to seek employment in the other industries of the district.

The managing director who lived at Velindre was Herbert Birch, a Mancunian who had connections with the Manchester Ship Canal. John James of St. Bride's Terrace was overlooker in the stone quarry; his son Alfred was a clerk there. At Abereiddi lived Thomas Thomas, engine driver.

The Irishman Philip Cronin, quarryman, still lived in Abereiddi. Andrew Gillies, brickmaker of Pentop, was one of three Scotsmen. Jabez Billison, granite quarryman of Porthgain Row, was one of two Lancastrians; George Cooper, brickmaker of Pool House, was one of two Yorkshiremen. Only John Hughes of Porthgain Yard came from North Wales.

There were others, mostly local men, whose family names are long associated with the quarries; Thomas Phillips of Abereiddi Street and his two sons – all stone quarrymen; David Harries, slate labourer of Porthgain Row; William Waters, slate quarryman and his two sons John (aged 14) brickwork labourer and George (aged 12) granite quarryman; the brothers David and James Salmon, blacksmiths, of Pentop.

At 4, Porthgain Row, lived the slate quarryman James James who had been associated with the quarries for some forty years. In March of the following year the entire community was appalled and distressed to learn of the murder of his daughter Mary and her four young children. Their throats had been cut and they had been buried beneath the kitchen floor of a cottage in Rainhill near Liverpool by Mary's husband Frederick Denning, a one-time seaman. A thief, philanderer and confidence trickster (as it was revealed) he, at times accompanied by his wife and children, roamed the world, often pretending to be the owner of several gold mines, relieving the unwary of their valuables. The Rainhill murders only came to light after his arrest in Melbourne for another murder; a crime for which he paid with his own life.

The tragic news was received by a community which already had problems of its own. In spite of the apparent prosperity all was not well. The rapid expansion of the company into a variety of different fields had over-stretched its resources. An appeal for extra capital was unsuccessful and a meeting of shareholders, held in August 1891, urged that the company should be wound up.

In July 1891, Charles Ogle Rogers of London, on behalf of the debenture holders (including John Davies, then of London) obtained an Order in the High Court of Justice, Chancery Division, against the *United Welsh Slate Company Limited*. By this Herbert Birch, managing director of the company, was appointed as receiver and was to act as manager on a temporary basis.

Writing to Messrs. Stevenson & Alexander, Solicitors, of Cardiff on 7th November, 1898, Herbert Birch stated that the *United Welsh Slate Company* had operated the quarries and brickworks at Porthgain between November 1888 and July 1891. During the first half of that time new works had been in progress. From July 1891 to May 1893 the Receiver had been in possession and work had only intermittently been carried on.

The *Pembroke County Guardian* of 12th September, 1891, informed its readers that changes in the company would not affect its business. It announced that the brickmaking machinery was in full operation, and that additional vessels were being chartered to fulfil large orders for bricks and granite. Two months later an advertisement appeared calling for smacks and other vessels to convey regular cargoes to Bristol Channel ports.

11. A three-masted schooner leaves Porthgain in the days of sail.

Their log books show that a number of locally owned ships were trading from Porthgain about this time. Destinations included Cardiff, Neath, Llanelli and Pwllheli and, more locally, Cardigan, Newport (Pembs.) and New Quay; unfortunately the cargoes are normally not specified. However in 1892 *Alice* took a cargo of slate slabs and bricks to Llanelli and one of granite chips to Cardiff. In 1893 *Sarah Ann* carried five cargoes of bricks to Milford, as well as two of granite and one of bricks to Haverfordwest; while *Martha Jane* carried two cargoes of bricks to St. David's and one of stone to Milford. Altogether over sixty cargoes were despatched from Porthgain in local ships during the year. The following year *Mary Ann* carried several cargoes to both Newport (Gwent) and Swansea; single cargoes of bricks and stones being recorded to Newport and of bricks to Swansea

On 8th July, 1893, it was reported in the local paper that a new company, the *Porthgain Granite, Slate and Brick Company Limited* had taken over the quarries and works. The principals, in what was virtually a private company, consisted of Herbert Birch and two or three other gentlemen. At that time the brickworks, at least, was closed, since on 7th October it was announced that the brickworks would open in about ten days, and that there was an immediate need for twenty workmen. Records of the Ecclesiastical Commissioners show that George Warren & Co. of Exmouth were granted sole rights of making bricks from the slate waste.

In 1894 the prospects of the *Porthgain Granite, Slate and Brick Company* were said to be good, and it was reported that the company had purchased the 230 ton steamer *Ben Nevis*. Herbert Birch had already announced the intention of the company to construct a wet dock (where ships would remain afloat at all states of the tide) at the upper end of the harbour. It was designed to accommodate three steamers of up to 150ft. length at the same time. The entrance lock was to be 30ft. wide and there would be about 10ft. depth of water at neap tide.

The reasoning behind the plan was to accommodate larger ships by increasing the depth of water at spring tides from 11 ft. to about 16 ft.. In addition the improved shelter would mean ships, particularly steamers whose iron hulls were not intended for grounding, could use the harbour for the whole year instead of only during the summer months.

Previously the largest steamers that could be handled were of about 150 tons, and there was sufficient depth of water for these on only about five days per fortnight. The new dock would enable ships of at least 200 tons to enter on neap tides and of up to 500 tons on the highest tides.

Grave doubts were raised both locally and nationally regarding the viability of the scheme. However the Porthgain Harbour Provisional Order was eventually published in the *London Gazette* of 29th November, 1895. An elaborate plan, covering much besides, its most significant feature was the intended construction of;

> "A wet dock, one third of an acre or thereabouts in extent, situate partly in the existing harbour or creek of Porthgain, and partly on land adjoining thereto."

To undertake the construction of the harbour a separate company was formed by Herbert Birch. This was known as *Porthgain Harbour Ltd.*. Its plans included the construction of railways, reservoirs, gas and electric plants and much else. Not surprisingly money was not forthcoming, and the dock was not built. Nor were many of the plans for development of the quarries put into effect.

An article on the slate industry in Pembrokeshire appeared in the *Pembrokeshire County Guardian* on 16th February, 1895. It attributed the bad reputation of the local slate to the poor quality of roofing slate obtained from the Porthgain quarry. Slate from the Abereiddi quarry was claimed to be more durable as Abereiddi slate used to roof the school at Llanrhian some forty years previously was still in good condition.

There were stated to be ample reserves of slate at Abereiddi for seven years without the necessity of further surface clearing apart from removing the overhang. In the previous week some 500 tons of this had been removed by the quarry manager, Mr. Jamieson, with the use of explosives. It was not proposed to work the flooded lower galleries of the quarry. Meanwhile it was the intention of the manager, Mr. Barber, to resume the production of slate slabs at the Porthgain quarry.

12. Abereiddi as it would have appeared c. 1900 at the end of its working life. The quarry buildings on the tramway level are more or less complete, with the row of quarrymen's cottages at the foot of the slope. The old village is in the foreground, with the tower on the headland above the quarry.

In his report to Messrs. Stephenson & Alexander, Herbert Birch stated that the *Porthgain Granite, Slate & Brick Co .Ltd.* had owned the property from May 1893 to August 1895. However, owing to shortage of capital the quarries had been only partially operating.

In August 1897 applications were invited from the public for sub-scriptions totalling £30,000 for expansion of the quarries and harbour. In the Francis Green Collection are cuttings from an unidentified financial publication. An article dated 16th March, 1898, describes the deficiencies of the location and nature of the harbour, and comments on the long and undistinguished record of the slate quarrying industry of Porthgain and Abereiddi. It remarks that operations during the previous year have been concerned mainly with brickmaking and granite crushing. It continues;

"The results even of late have not been particularly brilliant, as the concern, we understand, has for some time been run in the interests of the Debenture holders. The work projected by the *Porthgain Harbour Company* will no doubt benefit the owners of the quarries and brickworks, but unless the public are anxious to act the part of philanthropists to the concern, they will be well advised to keep their spare cash for more promising investment."

On 10th December, the same publication contained the following;

"Some time ago we reported that the harbour traffic depended almost entirely on the shipments to and from the Porthgain and Abereithy slate quarries and brickworks. How flourishing is the position of these works will be realised when we mention that they have practically been closed for the past four months."

In his report dated December 1898, Herbert Birch stated that, between September 1895 and February 1898, the quarries had been in the possession of C. O. Rogers. From July 1898 they had been owned by Birch, who had meanwhile sold the harbour to a new company.

The doubts were probably well founded. On 27th February, 1897, the local paper recorded the shipping movements at Porthgain during the previous week:

"*Westleigh* arr. 150 tons manure; *Pioneer* arr. 60 tons coal, loaded 60 tons macadam; *Jno James* arr. Ballast, loaded slates and bricks; *Alice* loaded macadam; total handled during week 430 tons."

About this time there were plans for the construction of a railway between St. David's and Jordanston, where it would connect with the *North Pembrokeshire and Fishguard Railway* which was then under construction. It was originally intended that the line should keep to the high ground passing through Croesgoch. Later a deviation was proposed by which the line was to pass through Trefin and Llanrhian. From the latter it was hoped to build an industrial branch to the harbour at Porthgain. On 8th October, 1898, the *Pembroke County Guardian* announced that the *St. David's Railway* was being pegged out and that a date for the formal cutting of the first sod would soon be announced. That ceremony would seem never to have taken place.

On 12th February, 1898, Herbert Birch reported that Charles Ogle Rogers had transferred all his property in the quarries to *Porthgain Harbour Limited* – the company controlled by Birch which planned the improvements. Contracts for the construction had been agreed and Mr. Barber had left Velindre.

In 1898 Herbert Birch became engaged in litigation with Messrs. Stephenson & Alexander, Solicitors, of Cardiff. The correspondence between them gives much information on the complicated state of affairs at Porthgain and Abereiddi during the 1890s.

Birch, who describes himself as Proprietor of the *Porthgain & Abereithy Quarries & Brickworks*, states that the quarries were altogether capable of producing up to 80,000 tons per annum. In its existing state the harbour was capable of handling only about a quarter of this. In practice the exports had never reached 10,000 tons for any 12 months during the 1890s.

Quoting the half-yearly figures, he attributes this largely to the lack of harbour facilities limiting the trade mostly to the summer months. This would be rectified by the construction of the wet dock able to handle the larger steamers (now replacing the coastal sailing ships) throughout the year. However it was stated that there had been exports to 12 principal English and 5 principal Irish ports as well as 29 Welsh destinations. In addition there were claims of sales to Holland, Belgium and America.

Years	Summer	Tons	Years	Winter	Tons
1890	April to September	730	1890/1	October to March	2957
1891	" "	3948	1891/2	" "	1830
1892	" "	2000	1892/3	" "	2663
1893	" "	1800	1893/4	" "	614
1894	" "	6067	1894/5	" "	2754
1895	" "	2703	1895/6	" "	2614
1896	" "	1720	1896/7	" "	1068
1897	" "	3239	1897/8	" "	1728
8	" "	22207	8	" "	13578

Total tonnages exported from Porthgain (April 1890 – March 1898).

The papers contain few references to individual cargoes and destinations during the period. However between 12th February and 2nd July, 1898, there had been altogether 12 shipments – mostly in local ships. Of these, six, totalling 432 tons, were of bricks to Cardiff, Pwllheli (2), Goodwick, Pembroke and Pembroke Dock. Five, totalling 197 tons, were of macadam to a variety of destinations around Milford Haven. There was a single shipment of 150 tons of slate for London - the largest individual cargo.

The London cargo formed part of only remaining contract for slate. At this time production amounted to about 6,000 slates per week. There were large stocks of slate slabs, for which there was apparently little demand.

The Porthgain bricks were exceptionally hard and suitable for industrial use as well as in construction. In addition to the main kiln, there were two much smaller circular kilns and a bluing kiln. However the Hoffmann Kiln suffered from faults which meant that it worked only intermittently, and there were problems with the quality of the production. Reconstruction of the kiln in 1896 proved only a partial solution and there was difficulty in selling the unfamiliar slate-based bricks. During 1898 the brickworks operated only for three months from March to May, producing an average of 30,000 bricks per week.

The granite quarry was equipped with a crusher capable of producing 70 tons of macadam per day. However, throughout 1898 the quarry was idle; there was no demand for setts and paving, while orders for macadam were satisfied from existing stock.

Steam engines were employed to drive the brickworks and the granite crusher. A water wheel was used to provide power to operate the machinery for cutting and planing the slate slabs, but could only operate for about two-thirds of the year. At other times a steam engine was used; it was suggested that if turbines were installed this would not be necessary; also power to run electric lighting would become available.

Tramways linked the various quarries and the brickworks with the harbour. No plan is included, but there is a description of the various lines, all of 3 foot gauge. There is also a list of the thirty or so trams and wagons of various types suitable for transporting, slates, bricks and other materials.

On the quayside was a fixed steam crane for loading the ships; the first travelling crane had not yet arrived. Also mentioned is a 4 horse-power oil engined launch called *Carol* which was used as a pilot launch and also as a tug for ships entering and leaving the harbour.

There is a detailed list of all the equipment and of all the properties owned by the company. Apart from Velindre there were two recently built houses at Sunnyside (one was occupied by the manager), the Sloop Inn and some two dozen cottages. At Abereiddi was the row of seven cottages and the house of the foreman. At Slate Yard there were three cottages and there were five (one larger than the others) at St. Bride's Terrace. There was also a cottage at Velindre.

In Porthgain there were five cottages and one house in Porthgain Row and five cottages (of which three were out of occupation) at Pen Top. Finally there was Pool House. Other than Sunnyside the cottages were mainly constructed of slate with slate roofs. The total value of the property was assessed at a little under £13,000.

In spite of the problems, a new phase was about to begin at Porthgain; the future would depend on its granite. The days of the export of slates were nearly over, though the brickworks still had a vital part to play in the story of Porthgain.

V; A Decade of Change
Porthgain (1900-1910)

Work on the long-awaited harbour improvements at Porthgain began in the spring of 1898. In February it was announced that the contract for the new dock had been let; the following month the contractors were advertising for workmen who were required immediately. However in July 1899, Herbert Birch was being sued by Cave & Co., the contractors, for non-payment for work carried out at the quarries.

In 1900 work was restarted, though the wet dock was never built. This time the plan was more modest and essentially involved the creation of the present-day harbour. A new central pier was to be constructed, dividing the harbour into two and forming a sheltered and almost totally enclosed inner basin. At the same time the western pier was to be lengthened.

On the western side of the harbour two berths were to be built; the more northerly 130 ft. and the other 150 ft. in length. These became known respectively as the Hadfield 'H' berth and the Baxter 'B' berth after the crushers which originally served them. South of these was what was known as the 'Wave Basin'. Most of the western quay was roughly parallel to the new central pier, though the southern section was to be built at a slight angle to this, while the wall in front of the brickworks was intended to have a sloping face. The reason was to reduce the tidal surge which could otherwise build up by waves being reflected back and forth across the harbour.

To allow construction to proceed at all states of the tide, a temporary wooden dam was built between the brickworks and the end of the western pier. On 11th November, 1900, Henry Roberts, who seems to have been in charge of the project, entered in his notebook;

"Got in first pile for dam at low tide."

By the night of 25/26th November the last pile of the dam was in place and the harbour was watertight. Work could then begin on deepening the harbour. This involved the removal of much silt and, at the upper end of the harbour, cutting away the underlying slate. On 6th December eleven men were at work excavating rock at the upper cutting in the harbour, while twenty-five others worked on the dam; two days later the foundations of the wave basin wall were being prepared. On Tuesday, 1st January, 1901, two steam cranes were at work on the new harbour.

Progress was not uninterrupted. During a gale on 5th March, waves washed over the dam leaving the cutting filled with three feet of water. On 13th April a telegram was received ordering all men to be paid off. Work restarted on 4th May, but two days later stopped again for some hours until the workmen received assurance about their wages. On 15th May the men withdrew their labour once more. On 27th July Henry Roberts wrote that he was leaving Porthgain for good.

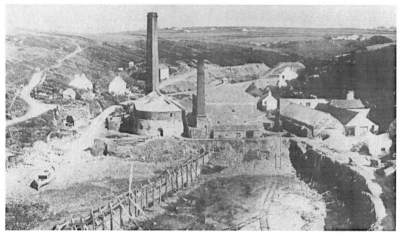

13. Porthgain Harbour under construction c. 1902, with coffer dam complete.

The contractors, Cook & Co., of Southampton, had other problems. In May 1901 they were successfully sued by Francis & Co. of London, cement manufacturers, for failing to pay for cement delivered. Cook maintained that the cement was of unsatisfactory quality; this claim was dismissed.

In spite of this, in January 1901, the *Porthgain Quarry Company* was advertising the sale of bricks, slates and slabs, while macadam would be available shortly. Meanwhile Herbert Birch, described as managing director of the *United Welsh Slate Company, Ltd.*, and promoter of the *Porthgain Granite, Slate & Brick Company (Ltd.)* was being sued for bankruptcy.

The 1901 Census shows Velindre was vacant, as were five of the seven cottages at Pentop and three of those at Abereiddi. Alfred James of 1, St. Bride's Terrace was 'Clerk in Brick and Slate Works'; Thomas Bowen aged 45 of Pool House was 'Engine Driver at Slate Quarry' while his teenage sons James and Edmund were respectively assistant engine driver and stoker. Nine others were referred to as slate quarrymen. Among them at 1, Pentop were John Hughes, a native of North Wales and his 26 years old son Samuel who was locally born.

There is no mention of men being employed in the brickworks or the granite quarry. Nor is there any reference to men being engaged on construction of the harbour. Housing developments had not started on the eastern side of Porthgain where there were only two inhabited dwellings.

14. Workmen constructing new harbour at Porthgain – early 1900s.

In the following year the property was put up for sale. The sale plan shows the partly built centre pier, as well as the temporary dam which is described as Lot 2. The purchasers were *Forest of Dean Stone Firms*, a Bristol company. Work on the harbour was resumed. By early 1904 this was complete and the harbour was again open to shipping. The new owners were particularly interested in developing the trade in roadstone, and the first of the giant dockside bins date from this period.

During the period of construction of the harbour a number of vessels arrived from Swansea and Cardiff, presumably with building materials. These would have been landed on the beach east of the harbour. Some, at least, was carried in local ships; these in return exported about twenty cargoes, mainly to Pembroke Dock and Swansea.

During 1904 the company quotation book suggests that there were shipments of slate slabs to Swansea and of bricks to Swansea and Dublin. Destinations for shipments of macadam seem to have included Folkestone, Ramsgate, Gloucester, Sheerness and Liverpool. More locally bricks were supplied to the military at Pembroke Dock and Dale and to St. Bride's for the rebuilding of Kensington House. One unusual quotation was for slate slabs for use as damp courses at Aberdyfi.

The Second Edition Ordnance Survey Map of 1906 shows Porthgain as it was in the last days of the production of slates and slabs. In the valley, the slate mill was no longer in use for its original purpose. Opposite was the brickworks, with its machinery shed, kiln and drying sheds. The brickworks, for a decade its extremely hard bricks had been perhaps the most significant of the products of Porthgain, was still busy; but by then much of its production was destined for the massive alterations which were taking place at Porthgain itself.

15. Slate Workshops and Brickworks with harbour nearing completion c. 1903. Slate Depot on Quayside near Pilot House before construction of Storage Bins.

The Abereiddi Slate Quarry had already closed, probably in 1904. However the tramway from there to Porthgain was still in existence though, apart from the section near the harbour, practically disused. The 3 foot gauge lines at the lower level were used largely for removing slate waste from the quarry, via the tunnel, to the brickworks and conveying the bricks from the kiln to the loading quays.

The harbour extensions were more or less complete, with the new centre pier and a modern quay with two berths for ships on the western quay. The old slate depot had been replaced by a row of brick-built storage bins for the rapidly developing granite trade. Capable of holding some 6,000 tons they had the disadvantage of not being able to transfer the granite directly into a ship's holds. Three short tunnels ran under the bins. Openings in their roofs allowed trams to be filled with stone; the trams were then pushed to the quay, where steam cranes emptied their loads into the ship. Alongside the new southern berth was a much taller row of storage bins – by 1906 there were eight of these holding upwards of 400 tons apiece. These bins were emptied through openings in their sides.

On the hill above the bins were the crushers which produced the graded roadstone on which the future prosperity of Porthgain depended. Pentop Row still stood, but otherwise almost all the buildings associated with the slate industry had disappeared; so too had the extensive system of tramways. Since 1887 the slate quarry had been deepened and widened, though its lower levels (as those at Abereiddi) were flooded, while the incline in the northern face had been filled with rubble.

Entirely new since 1887 was the granite quarry at Penclegyr, about half a mile west of the harbour. It was still relatively small; until about 1900 much of its production had been for paving and building stone. There were only a couple of buildings at the quarry; a smithy and probably a weigh-bridge. From the quarry a tramway – single tracked with two or three passing loops – climbed to a point near the old slate tips where it curved in a south-easterly direction. Near the slate quarry it divided into two branches, both leading to crushers set above the bins. The line, like all those around Porthgain, was still horse-drawn.

16. Quarrymen at Penclegyr Quarry c. 1905; over eighty workmen are included in the photograph.

The process of crushing the granite produced large quantities of granite dust for which there was little demand; most was tipped on the hillside above the old slate workshops. Much of the slate waste had been turned profitably into bricks; in the case of the granite dust an attempt was made to use it to manufacture concrete products.

17. Porthgain Village and Brickworks from south c. 1905. 'The Street' is on the left with the Abereiddi Tramway running in front. The Brick Kiln with its tall chimney is to the right of the Machinery Shed, with the low drying sheds in front. The Company Office is to their left. At the rear on the hilltop re the crushers, with the (still incomplete) row of bins below.

18. Porthgain Harbour and Brickworks c. 1905 from a point above the Pilot House. The Henllys Limekiln is to the left of the Brick Kiln with The Sloop and Sunnyside further along the road. Higher up the hill is the terrace of larger houses, the nearest of which is Glan-y-Mor. The old Slate Workshops are just visible to the right of the Brickworks.

Porthgain c. 1906

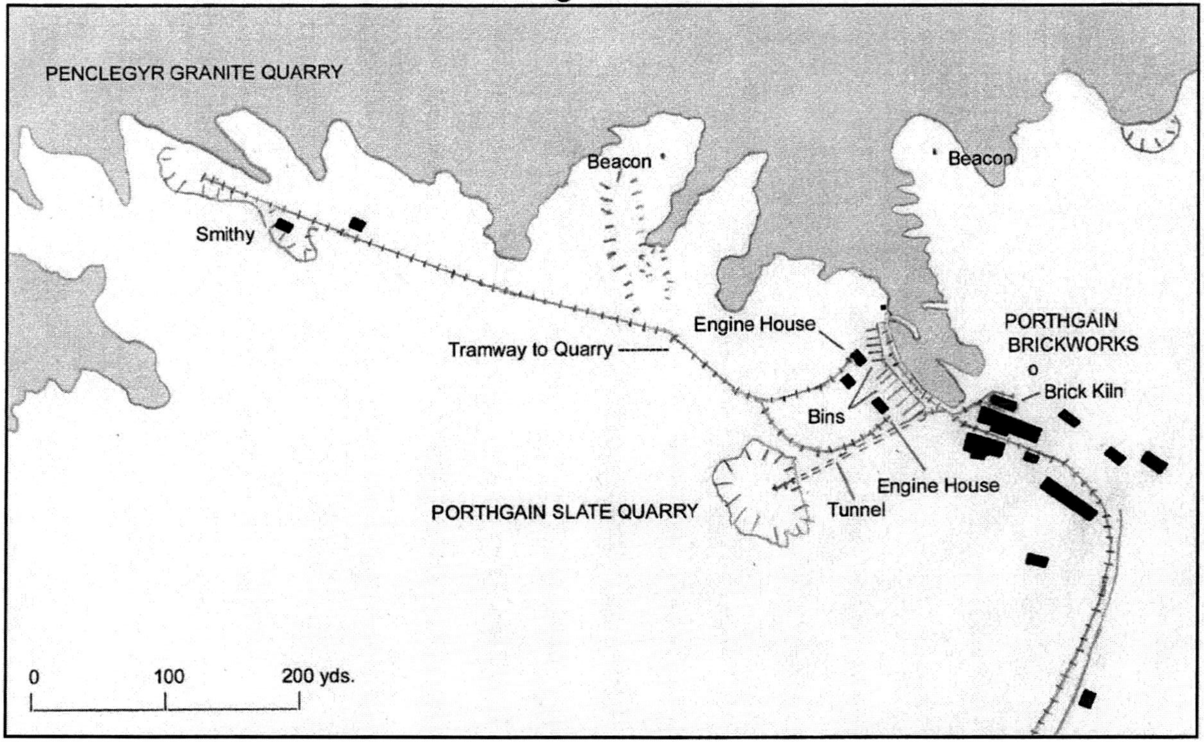

PENCLEGYR GRANITE QUARRY

Smithy

Beacon

Beacon

Engine House

Tramway to Quarry ———

PORTHGAIN SLATE QUARRY

Bins

Tunnel

Engine House

PORTHGAIN BRICKWORKS

o Brick Kiln

0   100   200 yds.

50

In the 1900s concrete flagstones were produced in a variety of sizes from 2ft.0in. x 1ft.6in. to 3ft.6in. x 2ft.0in.. Success was limited, although occasional shipments were made to destinations such as Briton Ferry and Llanelli. Production seems to have ended in June 1910. Almost half a century later the process was revived by the Salmon brothers, who successfully used granite dust extracted from the dumps to manufacture concrete blocks.

19. Porthgain Harbour showing Storage Bins under construction c. 1905. Isles Crane on quay. Slate Era buildings above Harbour have already been demolished. Stationary Engine at top of Incline. Entrance to Tunnel to Slate Quarry (visible at rear) on left of row of bins.

Work in the quarries was hard and at times dangerous. On Saturday, 24th February, 1906, John Hughes was killed as the result of an explosion. A careful and experienced workman and in charge of blasting, he had been, aided by his son Samuel, preparing a charge of gelignite to blast rocks in the granite quarry. The inquest recorded death as being due to misadventure.

A record of sales for October 1907 gives an idea of trade at that time. Sales of slates amounted to less than £14, slabs 2/-, bricks £79; all were entirely local. By contrast granite sales of £221 were almost all despatched by ship. Wages were £187; after allowing for other revenue and expenses there was a profit of just over £60 for the month.

The *Forest of Dean Stone Firms* had taken over some half a dozen stationary steam engines – some of them being of ancient vintage – as well as a comparatively modern steam crane from the previous owners. These, together with a water wheel, had provided power for the slate mill, the brickworks and the crushing machinery. In the succeeding years a number of engines were purchased, partly to replace some of the older engines, partly to power the new crushers which had been erected on the high ground above the west side of the harbour. In addition a traction engine and a steam wagon were provided to carry out local deliveries.

In 1905 traction engines were busily engaged in hauling bricks from Porthgain for use on the direct railway line from Clarbeston Road to Fishguard which was at last under construction. The heavy traffic caused considerable damage to the local roads and the Haverfordwest Rural District Council demanded compensation from the company.

20. Porthgain Street and Penrallt c. 1905 showing start of Abereiddi Tramway.
' Scotch Houses ' visible in distance beside Llanrhian road.

Among company records is a reference that between January 1904 and November 1909 a total of 1,084 vessels had been loaded at Porthgain; unfortunately most of the detailed records have been lost. However during the three months from June to August 1909 there had been 101 sailings totalling 12,897 tons. By the end of the decade trade was booming.

Surviving log books of local ships record exports to a variety of harbours in the south and west of Wales and a few to the Bridgwater area. But they amount to less than a quarter of the total shipments in the period and provide virtually no information on the cargoes carried.

Other records from 1909 show a stock of several thousand slates at the, by then closed, quarry at Abereiddi. These were later sold off locally.

Stored in the yard were nearly 600,000 bricks, with more than 100,000 remaining in the kiln. Nearly 200,000 had been used in 'new work' in the construction of the bins and various quarry buildings.

Before 1909 the trams used for carrying granite from the quarry to the crushers had been horse-drawn. By August 1909, in anticipation of the arrival of the first steam locomotive, the upper railway was being laid with heavier rails.

21. A busy Porthgain Harbour in days when sail still predominated – early 1900s

As it eventually developed the new system showed a number of differences from the original line. The upper levels of the quarry were approached, as before, via a shallow cutting. To reach the lower levels a new line was laid which ran alongside the cutting to the top of a steep incline leading to the lower quarry. An old traction engine was used as a stationary winding engine for raising the loaded trucks to the top from where the locomotive would haul them to the crushers.

Near the top of the incline was a range of brick buildings, including a blacksmith's shop, compressor house, stores and mess room. A new weighbridge was provided at the top of the cutting and, above the slate quarry, the locomotive shed which eventually held two tracks. The main line ran past the engine shed to a tipping stage alongside the crushers. A second line ran from the shed to the top of the incline leading to the quay; it was principally used to carry coal and other materials for use in the quarries. All these lines were of 3ft. gauge, as were others used for transferring crushed stones to the bins and for removing dust to the dumps.

In August 1909 the first locomotive arrived; an 0-6-0T, newly built by

Barclays of Kilmarnock, *Porthgain* was employed on the upper level. The stone was hauled from the quarry to the crushers in wooden tipping wagons, each carrying 4 tons, of which about thirty were purchased.

At first it seems that the locomotive ran a fairly regular schedule of hauling filled wagons from quarry to crushers at intervals of around a quarter of an hour. The train often consisted of only one or two wagons, the maximum length being about half a dozen; not the most efficient system of operation.

22. Quarry workers and wagons at Penclegyr Granite Quarry in pre-steam days.

On the lower level, side-tipping metal trams which held about a ton transported the crushed stone from the bins to the various loading quays. A steam crane (the Isles crane) which had arrived about 1900, was used for loading the ships. During 1909 the standard gauge craneway was re-laid and extended in preparation for the arrival of a second steam crane – the Grafton crane.

With no direct main line rail connection, Porthgain was almost entirely dependent on the harbour for its trade. *United Stone Firms* of Bristol (who had taken over *Forest of Dean Stone Firms* in 1909) acquired their own fleet of steamers to serve Porthgain and their various other quarries in Ireland and the West of England.

Five of these were new purpose-built steamers, each capable of carrying 350 tons of cargo. *Porthgain, Liscannor, Mountcharles* and *Dean Forest* were named after company quarries; *Multistone* was a company code name. In addition two smaller second-hand steamers *Volana* of 280 tons and *Hopetoun* of 100 tons were purchased.

During the early years of the twentieth century a number of new, privately-owned, houses were erected to provide accommodation for the increased workforce. These were built on the Henllys side of the valley. They were much larger and better equipped than the company-owned cottages of 'The Street'. Because of their south-west aspect they became known as 'Sunnyside'. Alongside the Llanrhian road a Workmen's Institute was constructed; this also served to accommodate workmen who did not live locally. In a village which produced four different building materials – slate, brick, granite and (to a lesser extent) concrete – the Institute was made of corrugated iron.

By early 1910 reconstruction was almost complete. The golden age of Porthgain was about to begin.

23. Abereiddi Terrace with sheep being dipped at rear of cottages.

VI; The Years of Prosperity
Porthgain (1910-1914)

In 1911, the new owners of Porthgain, *United Stone Firms*, issued a substantial volume which described their various undertakings. On the Porthgain Granite Quarries it reported:

"During the past few years they have been extensively developed and the quality of the prime beds now being opened up and worked has exceeded the most sanguine expectations. A Railway has been constructed to convey the Granite by locomotive from the Quarries to the Breakers, and the Quarries are equipped with a new and powerful compressed air plant for working the Drills and Machinery. An extensive Breaking Plant has also been laid down comprising Baxters, Broadbents and Hadfield's Breakers of the latest and most improved types, together with modern appliances for handling and loading the Granite with a minimum of hand labour.

A supplementary Plant has recently been erected to deal with the small gauges. By means of a Zimmer Conveyor all the surplus smalls are conveyed, elevated and put through a double set of Rolls, and special Screens of the most modern pattern, supplied and erected by Messrs. Ord and Maddison. This produces specially screened small gauges, perfectly clean and free from dust, which are stored separately in large quantities ready for shipment. The quality of these Screenings cannot be surpassed for Granolithic, Ferro Concrete, Artificial Paving and Stonework, and other uses.

Adjoining the Quarries is the Porthgain Harbour, which is part of the Freehold Property. Large Storage Bins have been constructed, and from which the Granite is loaded direct into vessels alongside. The harbour is capable of accommodating four vessels on each tide, and steamers of up to 400 tons carrying capacity are loaded daily. We possess our own fleet of steamers which assures prompt and regular supplies."

The crushed granite (the Company's description) was used mainly as roadstone for the construction of highways suitable for use by motor vehicles which were replacing horse-drawn transport. Enormous quantities were required for this purpose, and Porthgain's hard-wearing granite was in great demand in areas where such stone was absent. Bulk transport by sea was convenient and economic for delivery to counties bordering the Bristol Channel and the coastal areas of South-east England.

The method of construction of these roads had been developed by, and named after, the Scottish engineer McAdam for the earlier turnpike roads.

Essentially a macadam road was built up of a series of layers each consisting of stones of similar size, each layer being rolled in before the next was added. The foundation layer was made up of large stones, each succeeding layer using stones of progressively smaller size. The final layer consisted of small chippings which helped to bind the road together and provide a relatively smooth surface.

To produce these grades of stone, the crushed stone was in effect passed through a series of sieves of different sizes. The product at each stage was directed to a particular bin where it was stored, and from where it could later be loaded directly aboard a ship.

24. United Stone Firms' steamer being guided through the narrow entrance between the piers at Porthgain.

The earliest surviving bills of lading date from 1909. These and other records of ships entering and leaving the harbour (though incomplete) provide a fairly accurate account of trade from that date.

On 14th July, 1909, *Norseman* loaded 20 tons of chippings and 160 tons of 2in. and 2½in. granite for Bristol while *Tantalon* took on 240 tons of 2in. granite for Newhaven and *Garlandstone* 140 tons of 1½in. granite for Watchet. On 31st July *Norseman* (160 tons) and *Hopetoun* (90 tons) both sailed to Bristol with ¾in. chippings and *Bessie* to Haverfordwest with 30 tons 2in. and 30 tons 1½in. chippings. The series of bins (eventually there were fifteen) was necessary to store separately the wide range of sizes of stone produced.

25. Company owned steamers *Volana*, *Porthgain* and *Hopetoun* in harbour c. 1910, together with ss *Clwyd*, while another steamer waits outside.

The prospectus lists over seventy county, town and district councils to which Porthgain supplied granite roadstone. The great majority of these were coastal settlements from Cardigan to Southend, mostly situated along both sides of the Bristol Channel and the coast of South-east England. But there were others well inland including Cambridge, Bath, Glastonbury and Guildford. To supply these involved shipping the stone from Porthgain to the nearest suitable harbour, then discharging it into rail wagons for the remainder of the journey. This added greatly to the cost which would have been avoided if Porthgain had possessed direct rail access.

In the prospectus reference is also made to Porthgain Brickworks which had recently been improved; it was hoped to extend sales to Dublin and London as well as around the Bristol Channel. But of the oldest of Porthgain's exports – slates and slate slabs – there is no mention.

The promise does not seem to have been realised as far as the brick trade was concerned. During 1911 there were two shipments to Aberaeron and three to Llanelli; in the following January there was one to Haverfordwest. The final shipment of bricks (apart from a part cargo to Pembroke Dock aboard the *Thomond* in April 1912) appears to have been to Aberaeron on 28th April, 1911, aboard the *Hopetoun*. Three months previously the same ship had carried the last cargo of concrete flags to Briton Ferry.

Porthgain Brickworks was apparently unique in Britain in that the bricks were produced from slate waste. Normally bricks are manufactured from clay, which is effectively a mixture of finely divided limestone (calcium carbonate) and sand (silica). When fired in a kiln these fuse together to produce bricks hard enough for building purposes.

The slate waste at Porthgain and Abereiddi is stained a rust colour due to the presence of oxides of iron. When burnt in the kiln, these oxides and the silica present in the slate produced exceptionally hard bricks which were suitable for industrial use, being capable of bearing far greater loads than ordinary bricks.

However the bricks are considerably heavier than normal, adding to the cost of handling and transport. Porthgain was, in any case, far distant from any large markets. Also the cost of manufacturing the bricks was high and the process proved uneconomic leading to the closure of the brickworks after two decades of intermittent operation.

Although slate and slab production had ceased some years previously, the Porthgain Quarry was still being used as a source of shale. With the closure of the brickworks, the slate quarry was finally closed.

Worksheet for employees of Porthgain Brickworks January 1911.

26. *Porthgain* loading stone with the aid of the Grafton crane.

At the beginning of 1911 bricks were still being produced. There were between twenty-five and thirty men employed in the various tasks including quarrying the slate, through the mixing, burning and drying processes, to stacking the finished bricks. Stephen Crone (later the manager at Porthgain) was then in charge of the brickworks; the skilled brick burners were O. Williams and J. Watters. They were paid a weekly wage; the remainder by the hours worked, for most at a rate of 5d. per hour. Brickmaking probably ended in May of that year, although it was not until 1926 that the kiln was finally demolished.

By the end of 1911 granite quarrying was the only industry being carried on at Porthgain. Altogether some eighty men were employed in quarrying and breaking the stone, transporting it by rail, crushing and stocking it by size in the various bins and loading it into the ships. Among them were Syd Bowen, W. Reynolds and many others who had previously worked in the brickworks.

During 1910, the first complete year in which Porthgain was owned by *United Stone Firms*, there were some 330 shipments of granite from the harbour. In addition there were five shipments of bricks and three of concrete slabs. Most cargoes were for Bristol, the West Wales ports and West Country harbours such as Braunton, Bideford and Lynmouth. Other destinations included Newhaven, Margate, Whitstable, Faversham and Belfast, as well as Deptford and Greenhithe in London. The largest numbers of sailings were to Braunton (63), Newhaven (41), Bristol (32), Haverfordwest (20) and Newport, Gwent (19). In all nearly forty destinations were served.

Most ships arrived light, apart from those carrying coal to feed the engines and boilers at the quarry. Occasionally a vessel would bring cement or timber or iron rails for the company. The *Western Counties Agricultural Cooperative Association*, which established a store at Porthgain, used the harbour from time to time to import cargoes of coal or artificial manure, but imports were strictly limited. To make a profit vessels trading with the West Country would return via Swansea or Llanelli to pick up coal for one of the Pembrokeshire ports before returning empty to Porthgain. One of the most regular of these was the motor ketch *Bessie Clark*, one of many such West Country owned vessels involved in the trade at this time, which would arrive light from St. David's to load granite for Braunton. A fortnight or so later she would return to repeat the process.

27. A laden *Porthgain* leaves her home port.

By this time almost all the vessels calling were steamships or had auxiliary engines. But the summer months were still the busiest with forty-five shipments of granite in June and thirty-nine in July. February with only seven shipments was the quietest month.

The year 1911, which saw the final exports of bricks and concrete slabs, followed a similar pattern. July was the busiest month with thirty-nine shipments, followed by June and May, each with over thirty. December was the quietest month with eleven cargoes. Destinations were largely similar to 1910, Newhaven with fifty cargoes being the most important, followed by Braunton (35), Bristol (29), Milford (16) and Swansea (15).

28. Porthgain c. 1912 with three company ships in harbour.

In 1912 there was even greater shipping activity at Porthgain with over three hundred and sixty cargoes of granite being exported. The highest monthly total was forty-five for May, followed by forty-two in June. December with fifteen shipments and February with sixteen showed the least activity. The harbours of North Devon and Somerset together accounted for about a third of the cargoes, with another eighty odd shipments to the South Wales ports. South Coast destinations included Newhaven, Southampton and Rye, while London received no fewer than twenty-four shipments. A single cargo for Dublin was the only shipment to Ireland.

Daily output varied widely. Some days nearly 400 tons could be quarried and broken by the four crushers. More typically output would be between 250 and 300 tons, though there were days when bad weather, or the need for clearing quarry debris, or maintenance of machinery, meant that little or no quarrying or crushing took place. In mid-November 1912 work had to be suspended because of the sea washing up into the quarry.

In spite of this by the end of the month the bins were full and for several days there was no work. It was reported that some of the quarrymen were leaving the district. Throughout December the weekly output averaged less than 400 tons; most weeks saw only three or four days' production.

During the twelve months beginning with April 1912, the total output was almost 55,000 tons; the highest weekly total of 1,791 tons being in September. Except for weeks when one or more days were lost output was seldom below a thousand tons.

29. View of Crushing Plant and Storage Bins from above old Slate Workshops c. 1912. Sailing ship being loaded using Grafton crane with loco *Charger* on adjacent track.

Throughout 1912 developments at Porthgain continued. In April extensions to the harbour were being carried out, and measurements were being made for the construction of new bins: the bins at the southern end of the main block (Bins 1 & 2) date from this period. Unlike the rest they were largely made from concrete. During May a new crane line was being laid. In late summer two second-hand 3ft. gauge locomotives arrived. *Singapore*, a Kerr Stuart 0-4-2 tank engine, was intended to work alongside *Porthgain* hauling stone from the quarry to the crushers. In practice the new arrival proved too heavy for the line and on one occasion broke the weighbridge. As a result she saw relatively little use. *Charger*, a much smaller Bagnall built 0-4-0 tank engine, was destined for use on the dockside lines hauling trams laden with stone from the bins to the loading berths.

The standard gauge crane line ran from the end of the western pier, along the quayside, past the slate and brick workshops, ending up near the entrance to the village. Here it was hoped to join with a branch leading from the proposed St. David's Railway. Later a short spur was built to the centre pier. Along the quay wall the line was dual gauge, a third rail allowing use by the 3ft. gauge stock. A parallel 3ft. gauge line ran along the base of the storage bins, allowing the trams to be loaded from the bins. The loaded trams could be shunted by *Charger* to the berth where a ship was waiting, where one of the cranes would tip the stone into the hold. The quay lines connected with others to the slate quarry (via the tunnel) and to the centre pier. A winch operated incline allowed coal and other material to be raised from the quay to the upper level.

Despite the success of the quarries at Porthgain, in 1913 the *United Stone Firms* passed into receivership. The two smaller and older company ships *Volana* and *Hopetoun* had already been disposed of and during 1913 the more modern *Dean Forest* and *Liscannor* were also sold. Then, on 29th September, *Porthgain*, laden with roadstone for Barnstaple, sank after striking rocks in Jack Sound. Fortunately her crew escaped in their small boat. As a result only *Mountcharles* and *Multistone* remained in company ownership.

Shipments of granite from Porthgain during the early months of 1913 were significantly lower than in the previous year. Possibly this was linked with the financial difficulties of the parent company. Production figures for the early months of the year, though incomplete, show that the average weekly output was about 920 tons, the highest total being 1,397 tons in the week beginning 31st March.

Extract from Register of Shipping entering Porthgain 1913.

Records for 1914 are more complete. Until mid April the weekly total was usually considerably below 1,000 tons. Afterwards the weekly production was well above that figure, on three occasions exceeding 2,000 tons. The greatest tonnage recorded was 2,221 tons in the week beginning 13th July. During the first ten months of 1914 some 57,000 tons of granite were produced, the average weekly production being in excess of 1,320 tons. For the whole year, which included the early months of the Great War, total production was probably not far short of 70,000 tons.

30. Lower galleries at Penclegyr Granite Quarry c. 1912.

On 24th November, 1913 – a fairly typical day – altogether 325 tons of granite were quarried and crushed. In the quarry four men were quarrying rock, fourteen breaking the stone, while one man and two boys were drilling the rock. Loading the wagons involved fourteen men; there were two on the locomotive and three tipping the stone from the wagons into the crushers. Crushing and screening required fourteen men and loading into ships thirteen. The total workforce who mostly worked for 9-10 hours was eighty-four. Several others were directly employed at the quarries by a Mr. Harries for whom 139 tons of the total output were quarried. The remaining company employees were engaged in a variety of tasks including maintenance, clearing debris, trimming the bins and general labouring.

During the crushing of the granite large amounts of fine dust, for which there was little use, were produced. Some was used in making the private road from Llanrhian to Porthgain; this was closed once a year to show there was no public right of way. On 16th April, 1914, *Mary Jane Lewis* was loaded with 62 tons of dust, but such cargoes were rare. At first much of the dust was dumped on the hillside above the slate workshops, but this area was soon filled. On 14th May, 1914, the manager reported that a large amount of dust and small grades had been tipped into the slate quarry, filling a pit 40ft. deep below the level of the quarry floor. This would have comprised the lowest levels of the quarry which is shown as being flooded on the Second Edition of the Ordnance Survey map of 1906.

31. Locomotive *Porthgain* prepares to haul a train of loaded wagons from the granite quarry to the crushing plant.

By this time there was a growing demand for small chippings to provide a suitably smooth surface for the motor cars, with their pneumatic tyres, which were becoming increasingly common. Tar-and-chippings was becoming the normal surface for main roads. To increase production, during the early part of 1914 major extensions and improvements, including the erection of a new gantry, were being carried out on the chipping plant at Porthgain.

Around this time company records refer to work at the 'new quarry' and on 'rails for new quarry.' Presumably this refers to the lowest level of the quarry. In addition a new line was being laid for the removal of silt from the harbour.

Although the cottages at Pentop had been demolished, the company still owned over twenty properties which were rented out to employees. The manager Mr. Sant lived at Velindre, Stephen Crone at Sunnybank, overlooking the village. Lower down at Sunnyside were to be found J. Watters and W. Harries, the latter a fitter; most of the houses on the east of the village were privately owned.

H. Bennett, another fitter, lived in Pool House; David Salmon, blacksmith, at St. Bride's Terrace. In 'Porthgain Cottages', Slate Yard and 'Abereithy Terrace' lived many of the ordinary quarry labourers. At Abereiddi, Griff Phillips, David Phillips and Henry Phillips were next-door neighbours.

Towards the end of 1913 over eighty workmen regularly found employment at Porthgain. On 26th February, 1914, no fewer than 129 men and a boy are recorded as being employed at the quarries.

In days of booming trade not all the workmen could find homes of their own. Some walked from neighbouring villages, others took lodgings with quarrymen's wives. Some, unable to find lodgings, took up temporary residence in the Workmen's Institute. During the summer of 1914 as many as sixteen men, mostly Irish, lodged here, the weekly rent being 2s.0d.. Haverfordwest Rural District Council was already concerned about conditions in some of the cottages (particularly at 'Scotch Houses') and the company was forced to make some improvements. But the company was in financial difficulties and could not afford to build new homes, while the council did nothing to provide public housing.

For Porthgain the first few years of the reign of George V had been a time of continued prosperity. There had been brief periods of success in the days of slate and with the manufacture of bricks, but those dreams had faded. This time it seemed the future was assured. Elsewhere a train of events was unfolding which was to have disastrous consequences for Porthgain. But this time it was nothing to do with the quarry or its owners. An assassination in far off Serbia was to lead to the outbreak of what eventually became known as the First World War.

32. Locomotive *Porthgain* with train of wagons at crushers while steamship leaves harbour.

VII; The Great War
Porthgain (1914-1918)

The outbreak of the Great War in August 1914 seems initially to have had little direct effect on Porthgain. Indeed, during the succeeding months many men were being offered work in the quarries. Labourers could earn a minimum of 5d. per hour for a working week of 40 hours with the prospect of overtime working. More skilled men who could handle explosives were paid at 6d. per ton for breaking and loading. According to the manager J. A. Rice they could expect to earn 40/- per week.

Some of the applicants were local men, but many came from the industrial areas of South Wales, from Llanelli, Aberkenfig and Pontyberem. Others came from further afield, from Plymouth and Minehead in the West Country, and from Wexford in Ireland.

However on 8th March, 1915, the *Pembrokeshire County Guardian* reported that the war had seriously affected Porthgain. Several quarrymen had been dispensed with and it was rumoured that many more would be suspended during the following week. This was said by the manager to be due to a lack of available shipping.

By May prospects had improved and workmen were again being recruited. Shipping movements were back to normal, and in June no fewer than forty-nine cargoes of granite left Porthgain, along with a cargo of scrap for Swansea. The only really serious loss had been trade with London and the South Coast, particularly with Newhaven which had been for years one of the chief markets for Porthgain granite.

On 14th October a fatal accident occurred following the derailment of the locomotive *Porthgain*. John Evans of Sunnyside, a former miner aged 58, was one of several men attempting to get the engine back on the rails. Evans was using a rail as a lever when the support slipped. He was thrown to the ground, the heavy rail falling across his chest and causing his death.

Records show that during 1915 *Singapore* worked for only four weeks while *Porthgain* was under repair. Her unpopularity was due to her being too heavy for the existing track. Meanwhile *Charger* is documented as working with the cranes in loading granite into ships.

Over the winter months, ships were few and far between and little stone was quarried. A number of the men volunteered for military service. On 2nd February, 1916, almost all the remaining workmen were paid off. A week later the manager informed Head Office that, owing to labour troubles, the quarries were at a standstill. No ships were loaded that month and only four in March. As in the previous year trade improved during the spring with twenty-two ships calling in May and twenty-one in June.

The largest ship which called was the *Mountcharles* which carried 300 tons, while *Norseman* carried 190 tons. Most of the others were much smaller – vessels like the ketches *Democrat* of 105 tons and *Bessie Clark* of 70 tons. Their destinations were ports around the Bristol Channel – Bristol itself; Minehead, Barnstaple and Bideford in North Devon; in South Wales Cardiff, Barry and Swansea; nearer home Pembroke Dock and Milford.

By October trade was almost dead with only two or three ships per month. At 12 noon on 2nd December the men were paid off and the quarries closed, leaving only a few men to maintain the equipment. The local newspaper announced that a number of men had left by motor bus for Bristol, where they would remain for an indefinite period. This was considered to be a special privilege for the workmen. Once again the shortage of vessels was cited as the reason for the closure.

Coastal shipping was much affected by the presence of German submarines in the approaches to the Irish Sea and Bristol Channel. Many ships were sunk around the Pembrokeshire coast and U-boats were greatly feared. On 8th April, 1918 *Mary Grace*, bound from Hook to Pwllgwaelod with culm, "came in for shelter from submarine."

There was still demand for granite; the problem was transporting it to the markets. While the war continued there was no possibility of a rail link being constructed. Motor transport was in its infancy, and there was more urgent work for what lorries there were. And any contracts lost to other better situated quarries would be difficult to regain when hostilities did eventually cease.

For the remaining men times were hard. Most of them lived in company-owned cottages in Porthgain and Abereiddi, in St. Bride's Terrace and Slate Yard. Rents were low, in many cases only 10d. per week. Even so the men found difficulty in paying and many fell in arrears. When conditions improved in the early summer of 1917, the company agreed with the men that small amounts should be deducted from their wages. As the manager wrote to Headquarters; "We had them paid up very well until the works closed."

As in the previous year the three months from May to July 1917 saw the greatest amount of trade. In 1916 there were 58 shipments out of a total of 121; in 1917 there were 54 out of 103 for the year. However the number of shipping movements was only about one-third of that for the immediate pre-war years; the tonnage (most of the vessels involved were smaller) probably even less. The destinations were also much more local. West Country towns, particularly Bideford, still featured, as well as Cardiff and Swansea, but a large percentage of shipments was to various destinations around Milford Haven.

So it continued throughout the war years. During the winter only a handful of men would be retained to carry out maintenance and load the occasional ship which called; *Water Lily* for Haverfordwest, *Garlandstone* for Port Talbot. In early summer a few more men would be hired as limited production resumed, only for them to be laid off at the end of the season. Local demand for granite was small; in September 1917, Thomas Evans, surveyor, of Solva received 200 tons of 1½in. granite at 8s.6d. and 40 tons of 1in. at 8s.0d. per ton. The company was glad to sell off its remaining stocks of slabs and bricks.

By the end of 1917 only half a dozen men were employed by the Company at Porthgain. Stephen Crone (by then the only regular employee) had been transferred to Bristol. In the spring there was some improvement, but the year 1918 saw Porthgain at probably its lowest ebb since the beginning of the century. The surviving records (though incomplete) suggest that there were no more than seventy sailings during the whole of the year. Nearly a third of these were to Port Talbot, about a dozen to the West Country, and almost all the others to South Pembrokeshire.

Stephen Crone had returned but, by the end of the year, the only others permanently employed were David Salmon, blacksmith, and Syd Bowen, engine-driver. For the people of Porthgain the Armistice of 11th November, 1919 meant, not only the end of hostilities, but the hope for better times in the future.

Extract from Register of Shipping entering Porthgain 1913.

VIII; The Final Phase
Porthgain (1919-1931)

Peace did not bring immediate dividends to the quarries at Porthgain. Four years of comparative neglect meant there was much work to be done to restore the plant and machinery to good working order. The spring and early summer of 1919 saw fewer than a dozen men employed. By early June their numbers had doubled, a figure which remained steady until late October when all except four were laid off. During this period there had been some trade with the West Country, particularly Bideford, and with Swansea, but much the most important destination was Pembroke Dock.

While the works were effectively closed, the opportunity was taken for a complete survey of all plant and machinery. In the loco shed *Porthgain* was in good condition and *Singapore* fair. *Charger*, used for loading ships, was in the yard near the dock – she also required attention. Nearby were the two steam cranes; the Grafton was in good condition while the older Isles crane was in need of a thorough overhaul. Two of the four crushers were in good condition, the others in need of repair. The state of the remaining equipment ranged between useless and good.

The portion of the railway known as the 'Jerusalem Road' had been broken off by a storm. The damage was presumably at the bottom of the incline leading to the lower quarry – the two quarries were known to the men as 'Jerusalem' and 'Caersalem'. Before the lower quarry – with its harder stone – could reopen, the track bed would have to be rebuilt.

Once more the construction of a railway to St. David's seemed a possibility. Cllr. J. A. Price, addressing a meeting in support of the plan, stressed the advantages it would bring to the quarries. He stated that in the past 80,000 tons of stone per annum had been exported by sea, mostly during the summer months, and that on average 100 men had found employment. With direct rail access trade would be largely unaffected by the weather and he envisaged considerable expansion at Porthgain.

It was not until July 1920 that work restarted in earnest and most of the men were re-employed. A year later the number of employees had risen to about forty, a figure which did not alter significantly until the summer of 1922 when more men were engaged.

By the beginning of 1923 there were some seventy workmen employed at Porthgain, a number that would remain fairly constant for the next few years. But the heady days of a decade earlier would never be repeated, with production only about half of what it had been.

By 1920 all the ships owned by *United Stone Firms* had been sold. Porthgain was still almost wholly dependent on sea transport and, in 1921, two steamships – *Stertpoint* and *River Humber* – were purchased by men who had connections with Porthgain Quarries. The latter, capable of carrying 400 tons, was the largest of all the 'company ships', though neither was actually its property.

In the summer of 1924 a new station was opened by the *Great Western Railway* at Mathry Road on the main line from Clarbeston Road to Fishguard. This was the intended junction for the St. David's branch, under consideration at the time, for which the *G.W.R.* gave only lukewarm support. Unlike the previous plan, the line was intended to pass no nearer than Croesgoch, some two miles distant from the quarries. However, there was the possibility of a siding being built from Croesgoch to Porthgain.

33. Abereiddi Quarry from north-west c. 1920, after the quarry had closed, but before the channel had been blasted to allow access for boats. Most of the bank along which the tramway ran had already disappeared, suggesting it was largely artificial.

A direct rail link to Porthgain was more necessary than ever. The main line through the Treffgarne Gorge passed alongside the rival Treffgarne Granite Quarry and in 1925 a siding was laid into the quarry.

Even less helpful than the railway company were the members of Haverfordwest Rural District Council, who were unwilling to provide a grant of £1,500 for the purchase of land required for the line. As Mr. Crone wrote to Captain Macintosh, the Controller at Bristol;

"Disabuse yourself of the fact that Haverfordwest RDC look to the works at Porthgain with any favourable eyes. In fact from our own knowledge we believe they would like to see it closed down."

It was firmly believed locally that some of the councillors had interests in quarries in the south of the county. There was however at least one County Councillor who fought on behalf of Porthgain – Cllr. A. Owen Williams of St. David's. Of him Mr. Crone wrote; "This gentleman has always been a strong supporter of Porthgain products at council meetings and outside."

The new station did however provide the possibility of moving stone by rail. The company supplied a second-hand traction engine *Daisy* and a number of wooden trailers to haul stone the eight miles to a siding at Mathry Road. Pulling two trucks with a total load of 10 tons, the journey took about four hours, including stops to take on water and to allow other traffic to pass. When unloaded the return journey took about an hour less. In any case the iron-shod wheels caused serious damage to the road surface.

The use of a traction engine did not prove a success. The tonnage it could carry was limited; also by the summer of 1925 *Daisy* was in urgent need of repair as were the wagons. A second-hand lorry sent from Bristol was equally unsuccessful. It was frequently under repair and it too was soon withdrawn, leaving lorries owned by haulage contractors as the only link with the railway.

There were other problems. Because of the hardness of the granite the crushers were becoming badly worn. The elevators and conveyors which transported the stone were giving trouble. The trams and the rails on which they ran were in need of replacement. Requests to Headquarters fell on deaf ears. When replacements did arrive they were invariably second-hand and frequently little if any better than the equipment they replaced.

Several of the boilers which produced steam to work the machinery – some dated from the nineteenth century – were worn out or needed extensive repairs. Of the locomotives, the unsuitable *Singapore* was withdrawn in 1924; by then *Charger* needed attention and there was little work for her on the harbourside railway. Even *Porthgain* was frequently under repair. Requests by Mr. Crone for a replacement locomotive were turned down.

These difficulties were not apparent to a reporter from the *West Wales Guardian,* whose article appeared on 2nd February, 1925.

"Our representative paid a visit to the quarries this week and compared with his previous recollections of the place was astonished to find the workings had been so extensively developed. There was evidence all around of tremendous activity, and it came as no surprise to be informed that 5,000 tons of material had been exported from the quarries during the past month. Even this great output is likely to be more than doubled in the near future, for preparations are being made for completely modernising the quarrying machinery, and a special plant for producing chippings – for which there is an enormous demand – is being installed. A new quarry has been recently opened up, which getting under the old workings, will reach the best quality stone that can be produced in the county."

However, the writer commented on the fact that money spent on developments came from England, and that the authorities locally showed little interest in Porthgain; "being apparently ruled by vested interests in the small undertakings opened up from time to time by farmers and land-owners." He concluded that if transport facilities were improved there was sufficient demand for granite to support the employment of 200 workmen.

By September 1925 only two crushers were operating, the third having been shut down because the conveyors and elevators could not stand the load. During the five weeks beginning 1st August, 1925, a total of 5,322 tons of stone was produced; wages at 11d. per hour amounting to £940. For the equivalent period in 1914 production had been 9,569 tons; with wages at 5d. per hour the cost had been £875.

There were some who earned higher rates of pay. William Rees and Tom Cotton, carpenters; David Salmon, smith; John Davies, mason and L. Johnston fitter, received 1s.3d. per hour. Griff Phillips, loco driver; Syd Bowen, crane driver; Jim Salmon, handyman; James Harries, William Phillips, David Phillips and Jim Mathias, all quarrymen, were among those receiving 1s.1d. per hour. Those on weekly wages included William Harries, quarry foreman, who received £3.15s.0d., J. H. Maurice, clerk, £2.15s.0d. and John Rees, motor driver, £2.10s.0d..

For the week ending 27th April, 1926, stone breakers (who worked in pairs) received about £3.6s.6d. each and were among the highest earners. Apart from a few, presumably boys, paid at lower rates, the week's pay ranged between £2.6s.3d. and the £3.18s.4d. earned by labourer H. Jones. This was a week where men worked a full week and some earned considerable overtime. This was not always the case.

By the mid 1920s troubles in the coal industry, culminating in the General Strike of 1926, were having an adverse effect on the output from the quarry. Much of the coal that was available was of poor quality and, at times, the supply dried up completely. As a result the company was sometimes forced to close down production for days on end.

The year 1926 did bring some good news to Porthgain. Since 1913 the parent company *United Stone Firms* had been in the hands of a receiver. However in October 1926 the company was taken out of receivership, reorganised and reconstituted. The new company, *United Stone Firms (1926) Limited*, was still based at Bristol.

Although brick making had ceased more than a decade previously, the brickworks buildings were still more or less complete, though most of the machinery had been sold as scrap. It was not until the summer of 1925 that work began on dismantling the kiln itself; its chimney survived for more than a quarter of a century. The machinery shed and the drying sheds were put to other uses in connection with the granite trade.

34. Porthgain Harbour c. 1928 after demolition of the Brick Kiln, but before the alterations to straighten the Baxter Quay and shorten the Centre Pier. Work in progress on Washing Plant.

The arrival of the relatively large steamers *Stertpoint* and *River Humber* in 1921 had suggested the possibility of recapturing some of the lucrative pre-war trade with London and the South Coast. Shipping records for this period are incomplete, but in August 1923, *River Humber* carried 300 tons of granite to Shoreham. October saw another cargo for Gosport.

During 1924 there were some 160 shipments of granite from Porthgain. However, apart from a further three cargoes for Shoreham, all were destined for thirty-three different destinations in West Wales and around the Bristol Channel. Of these Barnstaple, Bridgwater, Aberaeron and Haverfordwest each received more than a dozen shipments. Four ships departed for Fishguard and five for Solva, both only a few miles distant – testimony to the lack of a rail link to Porthgain.

Over the next few years the annual number of shipments remained fairly constant at about one hundred and fifty. The trade with South-east England was not recaptured and in 1926 the steamers *Stertpoint* and *River Humber* were sold. However in 1926 two cargoes were exported to Chichester, while the following year there was a single cargo for London.

A considerable number of these shipments were destined for wharves in towns and villages many miles from the sea – Carmarthen, St. Clears, Cresswell Quay, Cardigan, and (in Somerset) Dunball and Combwich as well as Bridgwater itself. Some of these, and open beaches such as Laugharne and Sandy Haven could only be reached on spring tides by motor ketches like *Democrat* which could carry no more than 100 tons of cargo.

At the beginning of 1927 ominous tidings were received at Porthgain. A letter to the manager stated; "The History of Porthgain does not justify any improvements or developments." The author of this statement was Walter Bryant who was managing director of the newly formed *United Stone Firms (1926) Limited.*

By this time the demand for the larger sizes of granite was greatly reduced. The old system of building macadamised roads by using layers of stone of various sizes had been replaced by the use of smaller chippings, bound together with tar, to give a smoother, hard wearing surface. In November 1927 Crone wrote to Headquarters;

"It appears to me that our macadam trade is doomed. I therefore think that we ought to go in for a chipping plant that would do the necessary with less steam and dust."

The local manager was a skilled practical engineer, far sighted enough to realize that if Porthgain was to succeed major improvements were essential. Among his suggestions was that the crushers should be removed from their position above the harbour and replacements erected at the quarry itself. This would greatly reduce transport costs and solve the problem of disposal of the dust.

He also proposed to deepen the harbour and lengthen the main loading berth so that larger ships could be handled; by this time plans for a direct rail link had been abandoned. To improve access to the harbour he advocated shortening both the centre and western piers. Ideally he considered that the construction of a new breakwater on the western side of the harbour some 200 feet beyond the existing pier would make the harbour safer and enable even larger vessels to be loaded.

The company was at this time unable to raise the capital required for these improvements. Where possible machinery was repaired or second hand equipment brought in from other quarries. By May 1929 the sole remaining operational locomotive *Porthgain* was worn out, and a second hand replacement, the Hudswell Clarke 0-4-0 tank engine *Newport* was purchased: a much-travelled locomotive she had at one time worked in Singapore, while

Singapore (and *Charger*) had been no further than Ireland. The powerful, though relatively light, *Newport*, with its short wheelbase, proved to be very suitable for the sharp curves on the line. *Porthgain* was withdrawn from service; repairs would have cost as much as the purchase of a good second hand locomotive.

Production was by now concentrated on the lower quarry. The loaded wagons were hauled to the top of the quarry incline by a stationary engine. From here the locomotive hauled them, via the weighbridge, to the crushing stage where their load was tipped and conveyed to the crushers. The wagons were made up in sets of seven. At any one time one set was being loaded, another unloaded, while a third was in transit. The fourth set was spare and might be used once a day.

35. Porthgain Village c. 1930 showing standard gauge rails running in front of 'The Street'.

At this time a typical day's production was around 150-160 tons of granite. During 1928 and 1929 some two-thirds of shipments were to Bristol and the ports of Somerset and North Devon; the remainder being to destinations in South and West Wales. In all nearly 180 shipments were made in the latter year, a small, but significant, increase on the preceding years. At times in the spring and summer the harbour was busy. On 26th April, 1929, *Eddie* loaded 220 tons for Bristol, *Teifi* 220 tons for Ilfracombe, *Democrat* 100 tons for Pembroke Dock, *Bessie Clark* 70 tons for Braunton – all chippings of various sizes – while *Agnes* carried 100 tons of 2½in. granite, also for Braunton. It must have seemed like old times.

During 1930 a number of major schemes for improving the arrangements at the quarries were put into operation. By then the old dust tip at Pentop was full and the surplus was being tipped into the sea at Aber Tunnell. This was causing a problem with silting at the harbour. It was decided to use the old slate quarry as a dust dump. A shallow cutting to accommodate a tramway was dug from the crushing plant to a point above the slate quarry. This proved expensive as the rock was harder than expected and a bridge to carry the railway from the top of the incline to the locomotive shed had to be provided.

At the same time the line extending from the tunnel into the slate quarry was roofed over. Metal shutters in the roof allowed trams to be loaded with dust (for which there was a limited demand) and taken back through the tunnel to the quay where the dust was loaded into waiting ships.

More significant was a plan to deepen the harbour by removing the accumulated silt and cutting away some of the underlying slate. The debris was to be removed to a tip on the hill to the east of the harbour. During May 1930 a 2 foot gauge tramway was being laid from the Centre Pier to this tip; the old traction engine *Daisy* being used as a stationary engine to work the incline.

To accommodate the larger vessels which could enter the harbour, the main (Baxter) berth was extended by straightening the quay wall at its southern end. This created a quay 210 ft. in length capable of handling vessels of 600 tons burden. At the same time the centre pier was shortened to provide a wider entrance to the inner harbour.

While these alterations were in progress no vessels could enter the harbour. Production of granite was suspended, some of the men being transferred to renovation of the plant. On 12th February, 1931, Stephen Crone wrote to Bristol;

"We have been stopped now nearly 6 months but have a gang of 30 on Harbour and bin extensions and plant repairs. The directors have been talking about shifting the whole lot of machinery to the quarry end where it can be concentrated and made more economical to run. They have talked long and talked much, if they had kept clear I would have shifted the lot and said nowt about it."

Had the crushers been moved, the line to the crusher stage would have become redundant. A new line from a point near the weighbridge joining the existing track above the bins would have enabled crushed stone to be unloaded directly from the wagons into the bins. It would also have cured the problem of dust contaminating the stone chippings.

On the evening of 3rd February s.s. *Florence* had sailed for Ilfracombe with 180 tons of cargo. It seemed that the future of Porthgain was assured. By mid March work on the new quay was complete. Among the first ships to use it were *Lady Thomas* for Weymouth on 23rd March and *Barchan* for London on 6th April. By the beginning of May daily production was around 200 tons with sixty-five men employed.

May saw seventeen shipments, including two to Littlehampton and one to Dover; the latter being of 460 tons aboard *Brightside*. During the following month there were twenty cargoes, all destined for South Wales or the Bristol Channel. July started promisingly, in the first four days three ships departed for Carmarthen and one each for Ilfracombe, Llanelli and Bristol. But they were the only sailings during the month.

By the early part of 1931 the company was again in severe financial difficulties. As a result *United Stone Firms (1926) Limited*, like its immediate predecessor, passed into the hands of the receiver.

On 23rd July, a letter despatched by the receiver informed Mr. Crone that all work was to cease immediately and that he was to make an inventory of stocks and stores. All sixty or so employees, with the exception of the clerk, were to be laid off, though a few might be taken on temporarily as a loading gang to complete existing orders

For the inhabitants of Porthgain the news must have come as a hammer blow, just when it seemed prospects were about to improve. But the quarries had encountered similar difficulties in the past, and had survived. The quarrymen could only hope the same would happen this time.

36. Porthgain Harbour – early 1930s after the straightening of the main quay and the shortening of the Centre Pier to allow access for larger ships.

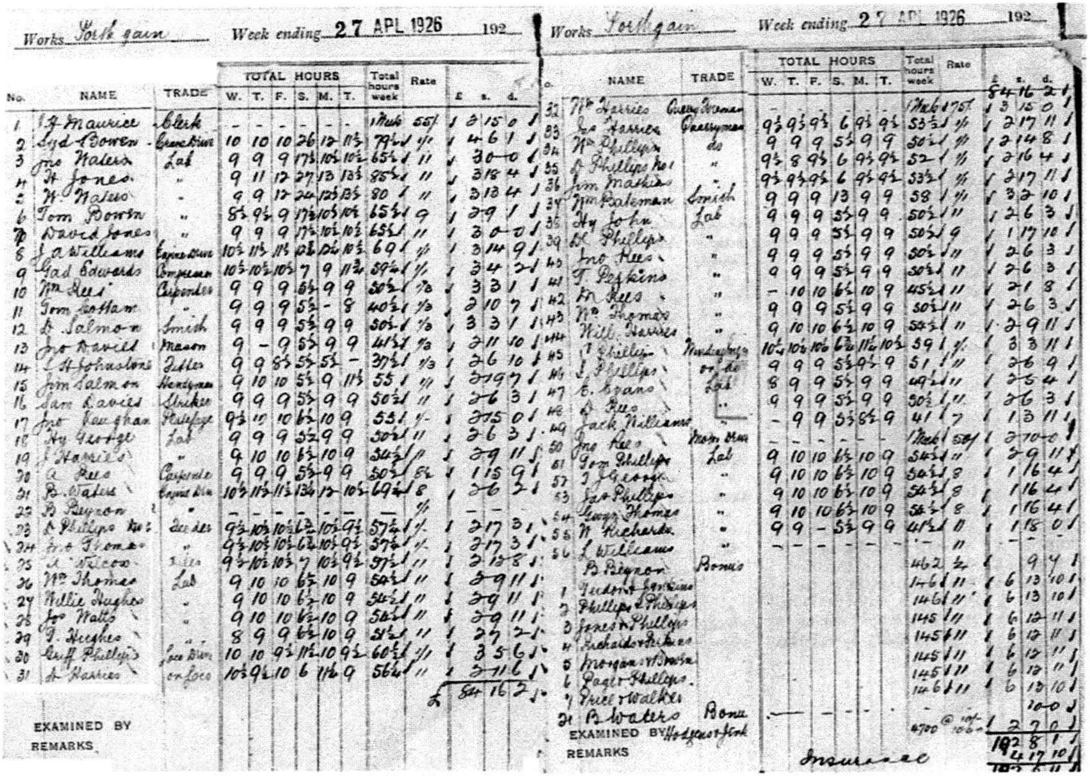

Works Porthgain Week ending 27 APL 1926 192

No. | NAME | TRADE | TOTAL HOURS W. T. F. S. M. T. | Total hours week | Rate | £ s. d.

EXAMINED BY

REMARKS

Works Porthgain Week ending 27 APL 1926 192

No. | NAME | TRADE | TOTAL HOURS W. T. F. S. M. T. | Total hours week | Rate | £ s. d.

EXAMINED BY

REMARKS

Wages sheet of workmen at Porthgain April 1926.

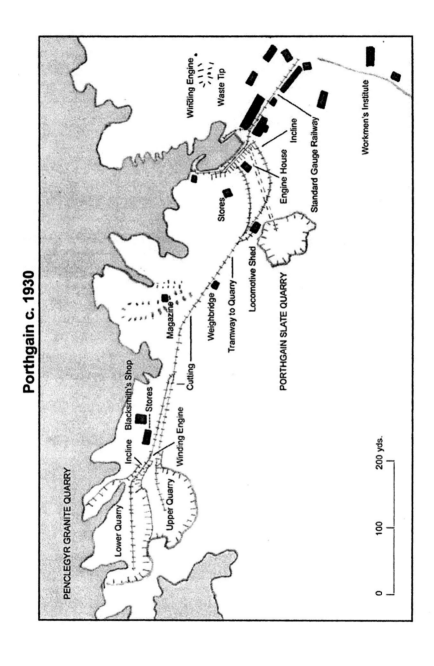

IX; Aftermath
Porthgain (1931-1955)

Although quarrying at Porthgain ended on 23rd July, 1931, considerable stocks of crushed stone remained in the bins, and the company held several uncompleted orders. A handful of men found occasional employment, loading those ships which came. They were paid only for the hours worked, which often amounted to less than a full day; and there was no guarantee when the next ship would arrive.

Iron Duke was the first; on 2nd August she loaded 145 tons of chippings for Bristol. On 3rd August, *May* took on 300 tons for Dover and *Cargan* 250 tons for Highbridge. The following two days saw two more ships sailing to Bristol. However during the remainder of the month there were only two further sailings to Bristol and one to Pembroke Dock.

September saw two departures for Bristol; during October no ships called, while in November two ships sailed to Swansea and one to Bristol. The final cargo for 1931 was despatched on 19th December when *Tanny* loaded 150 tons for Ilfracombe. Otherwise the second half of 1931 saw only the occasional lorry being loaded for local delivery.

On 18th January, 1932, the motor vessel *Westland*, described as, "a Dutchman who is trying to scrape a living around our coasts" arrived to load 140 tons ¼in. and 450 tons of □in. to dust; sailing to Erith two days later. The employment this provided was minimal; Syd Bowen (crane driver) received £1.15s.2d., and L. Jones £1.10s.3d., six others worked for between two and seven hours at 11d. per hour.

Apart from the landing of a cargo of phosphate from s.s. *Staffa* on 6th April there are no other records of vessels arriving during the year. The only other activity was the despatch of the occasional lorry load of dust which provided some employment for one or two men like J. Williams and W. Bateman. By September even this had ceased.

Stocks of crushed stone had become exhausted, but vast quantities of dust remained in the dumps. On 31st May, 1933, *Iron Duke* loaded a cargo for an undisclosed destination and again one or two men were employed loading lorries. There were prospects of selling the dust for the production of concrete. In late September seven men were taken on for a short time to prepare tramways for removing granite dust from the dump in the old slate quarry to the quayside.

On 2nd May, 1934, *Drumlough* loaded 270 tons (described as ¼in. to dust) for Liverpool. A fortnight later *Eleth* took aboard 335 tons, while on 24th October the much larger *Jeanette* loaded 575 tons for Deptford. It seemed that there was hope for this trade at least. However there were complaints that some of the dust had caked and was not suitable for the production of concrete.

37. Harbour entrance from platform overlooking storage bins, showing dual gauge railway on Western Pier. The rusting tram has not moved since the day the quarry closed in 1931.

These ships provided work for about two dozen men, although for only one or two days at a time. On 14th November *Bergendal* (a Dutch ship whose home port was Rotterdam) loaded 565 tons. Finally on 21st November, *Jeanette* returned. As far as can be ascertained, this was the final shipment from the harbour at Porthgain.

Throughout 1935 the only activity was the loading of lorries with dust. That, and the essential repairs to machinery and buildings, provided occasional employment for J. Williams, W. T. Rees, H. J. Jones and Francis Harries.

Then, on 31st July, 1936, the following announcement, promising a major development at Porthgain, appeared in the *Pembroke County Guardian.*

"Early developments are anticipated in the little North Pembrokeshire town of Porthgain, which is situated on the coast between St. David's Head and Strumble Head.
Porthgain's stone quarries have been noted for their excellent quality for generations. They have now been purchased by a big road engineering firm, and it is stated on the highest authority that in the very near future about 200 men will be employed at the quarries.
Transport of the stone obtained from the quarries is by sea and in connection with this traffic the harbour at Porthgain is also likely to be developed."

38. Ex-quarrymen and other inhabitants of Llanrhian Parish celebrate the Silver Jubilee of King George V in 1935 outside the Workmen's Institute; ruined Pool House on right.

The purchasers of the works at Porthgain were *London Crushed Stone Co. Ltd.*. Like their predecessors they lacked the capital for reopening the quarries and the hoped-for developments never took place.

In 1937 work began on construction of the Royal Naval Armaments Depot at Trecwn. There was demand for enormous quantities of stone, brick and cement – much of which Porthgain could have supplied – but it was others like Treffgarne Quarries and Goodwick Brickworks which benefited. However, many of the Porthgain quarrymen did find work at Trecwn – at first in construction and later in the production of weapons for the Royal Navy.

The Abereiddi Quarry had long been closed, and, during the early 1920s, a narrow passage had been blasted from the sea to allow small craft to use the flooded quarry as a harbour. In January 1938 a disastrous storm flooded the street of cottages, causing major damage. At the same time the village was struck by an outbreak of typhoid. As a result the row of cottages was abandoned and its inhabitants moved elsewhere.

With the outbreak of the Second World War on 3rd September, 1939, there seemed to be the possibility of the Porthgain Quarries playing their part in producing building materials for the many airfields and other military installations constructed in Pembrokeshire. Mr. Crone suggested the possibility of re-establishing the brickworks – it came to nothing – the manager's comment was, "the authorities seem in no hurry to finish the war." During the early war years much of the rail network and most of the equipment, including the Isles crane, were removed for scrap.

In 1942 the construction firm *George Wimpey,* who were building the aerodrome at St. David's, considered reopening the granite quarry, but, after removing one of the slate tips, they opened their quarry alongside the existing Penberry Quarry. The thousands of tons of dust remained largely undisturbed until after the war when the brothers Wilfred and James Salmon used some of it in the manufacture of concrete blocks.

Under the title *Porthgain Village Industries* Porthgain came under a succession of owners, the last being *G. B. Stein Refractories* of Sheffield. In the post war years the County Development Plan considered Porthgain Granite to be eminently suitable for use as roadstone.

However, with the quarries being within the area of the National Park, industrial development was not considered as being desirable. Eventually, after negotiations with the *Pembrokeshire Coast National Park*, the property was sold; the cliff top, including the quarries, being acquired by *The National Trust*, while the houses were purchased by their occupiers. A century and a half after they were built, renovated and re-roofed with Caernarfon slate salvaged from a wreck, today they are a fine example of the restoration of industrial housing of the Victorian era.

39. The 'Blue Lagoon', the flooded Slate Quarry at Abereiddi, hides some of the remaining mysteries of the industries of Abereiddi and Porthgain beneath its hundred foot deep waters. Before the quarry was opened to the sea, the tramway ran from the ruined Engine House on the far side of the quarry on level ground which has now disappeared, partly due to erosion and partly due to blasting. The tramway was used to carry slate to the harbour at Porthgain.

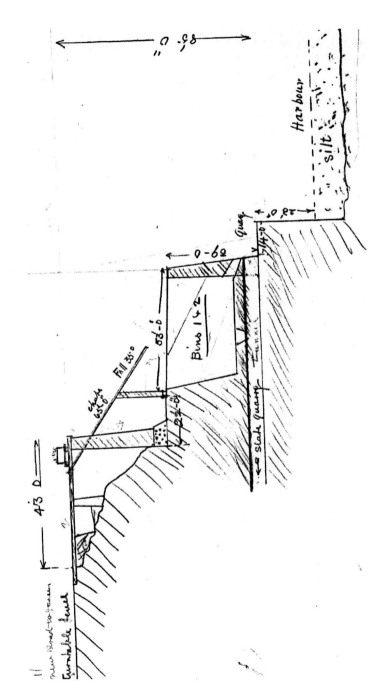

Section showing arrangements for tipping granite into storage bins and for loading ships at Porthgain; A S D Crone 1931.

Porthgain Exports

SLATES & SLATE SLABS

Aberavon, Aberystwyth, Annan, Ayr, Bristol, Cardiff, Carmarthen, Dundalk, Dundee, Fraserburgh, Garston, Giltar, Gloucester, Liverpool, Llanelli, Llangwm, London, Milford, Nairn, Newhaven, Newport (Mon), Pembroke Dock, Penarth, Portsmouth, Runcorn, Saundersfoot, Shoreham, Swansea, Waterford, Wexford.

BRICKS

Aberaeron, Arklow, Barry, Bristol, Cardiff, Cardigan, Castle Pill, Dale, Dublin, Fishguard, Goodwick, Haverfordwest, Llanelli, Llangwm, Milford, Newport (Mon), Newport (Pembs), New Quay (Cards), Pembroke, Pembroke Dock, Pwllheli, St. Bride's, St. David's, Swansea.

GRANITE

Aberaeron, Angle, Appledore, Avonmouth, Barnstaple, Barry, Belfast, Bideford, Blackpool, Blackpool Quay, Braunton, Bridgwater, Bristol, Briton Ferry, Bude, Burnham-on-Sea, Burry Port, Cardiff, Cardigan, Carmarthen, Castle Pill, Chichester, Combe Martin, Combwich, Cresswell Quay, Dale, Deptford, Dover, Dublin, Dunball, Erith, Faversham, Fishguard, Folkestone, Fremington, Gloucester, Goodwick, Gosport, Grays, Greenhithe, Haverfordwest, Highbridge, Hook, Hove, Ilfracombe, Instow, Ipswich, Landshipping, Laugharne, Littlehampton, Liverpool, Llanelli, London, Lydney, Lynmouth, Margate, Milford, Minehead, Neath, Newhaven, Newport (Mon), Newport (Pembs), New Quay (Cards), Newquay (Cornwall), Neyland, Nolton, Oystermouth, Pembroke, Pembroke Dock, Penarth, Picton Ferry, Poole, Port Talbot, Porthcawl, Portland, Portsmouth, Ramsgate, Rochester, Rye, St. Clears, Sandy Haven, Saundersfoot, Sharpness, Shoreham, Solva, Southampton, Strood, Swansea, Tapley, Tenby, Thames, Watchet, Watermouth, Weston-super-mare, Weymouth, Whitstable, Woolwich.

CONCRETE FLAGS

Briton Ferry, Llanelli.

CARGO UNSPECIFIED

Aberporth, Broad Haven, Lawrenny Quay.

....

The above list has been derived from Company Records and pre 1910 from a variety of sources such as Newspapers and ships' Log Books.

Bibliography

FENTON, R. S.; *Cambrian Coasters*. (Kendal, 1989).
GEORGE, Barbara; *Pembrokeshire Sea-Trading Before 1900*, (London, 1964).
JERMY, R. J.; *The Railways of Porthgain and Abereiddi*, (Oxford, 1986).
LEWIS, Roy; 'Halcyon Days of a Quarry Harbour of History' – Then and Now, No. 593, *Western Telegraph*, (15th December, 1993).
LEWIS, Roy; 'Abereiddi and Porthgain', *Cymru a'r Môr – Maritime Wales*, No. 23 (Caernarfon, 2002).
RICHARDS, A. J.; *The Slate Quarries of Pembrokeshire* (Llanrwst, 1998).
ROBERTS, Dafydd; 'The Pembrokeshire Slate Industry', *Pembrokeshire County History IV*, (Haverfordwest, 1993).
ROBERTS, Tony; *About Porthgain*, (Abercastle, 1996).
TUCKER, G. & M.; *The Slate Industry in Pembrokeshire and Neigh-bouring Counties*, (unpublished manuscript, Haverfordwest Record Office).

Newspapers and Periodicals
Carmarthen Journal.
Pembrokeshire Herald.
Haverfordwest & Milford Haven Telegraph.
Dewsland & Kemes Guardian.
Mining Journal.

40. Porthgain Quarrymen photographed outside the Workmen's Institute.